Y0-DEV-540

LIBERTY *vs.* EQUALITY

THE MACMILLAN COMPANY
NEW YORK · BOSTON · CHICAGO · DALLAS
ATLANTA · SAN FRANCISCO

MACMILLAN & CO., LIMITED
LONDON · BOMBAY · CALCUTTA
MELBOURNE

**THE MACMILLAN COMPANY
OF CANADA, LIMITED**
TORONTO

LIBERTY *vs.* EQUALITY

BY

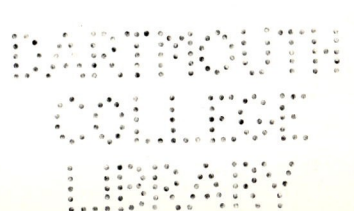

WILLIAM F. RUSSELL

NEW YORK
THE MACMILLAN COMPANY
1936

Copyright, 1936, by
THE MACMILLAN COMPANY.

All rights reserved—no part of this book may be reproduced in any form without permission in writing from the publisher, except by a reviewer who wishes to quote brief passages in connection with a review written for inclusion in magazine or newspaper.

Set up and printed. Published February, 1936.

PRINTED IN THE UNITED STATES OF AMERICA
NORWOOD PRESS LINOTYPE, INC.
NORWOOD, MASS., U.S.A.

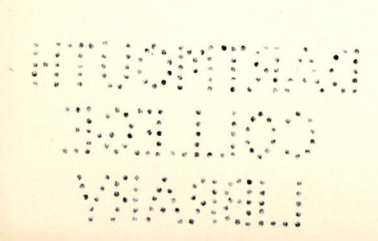

TO

C. D. R. AND J. E. R.

"Si l'on recherche en quoi consiste précisément le plus grand bien de tous, qui doit être la fin de tout système de législation, on trouvera qu'il se réduit à deux objets principaux: la liberté et l'égalité . . ."
    J. J. ROUSSEAU, *Du Contrat Social*, II, 11.

"If we were to inquire into what precisely is the greatest good of all, into what should be the purpose of all government, we should find it reducible to two chief objects,—liberty *and* equality."

To the Reader:

The idea of this book comes from a program of study that I have followed for several years. In trying to understand certain political and social problems as they affect education, I have been forced to ask the questions: "What are American ideals?" "What kind of a country did Washington and Jefferson want to found?" "Would Franklin and Hamilton have been pleased with the United States today?" "What was 'the American Dream'?" I tried to find an answer. I started with the usual American histories. I read everything I could find in the writings of Franklin, Thomas Paine, Washington, Hamilton, De Witt Clinton, Patrick Henry, John Adams, Jefferson, Madison, Monroe, Henry Clay and Abraham Lincoln. Their ideals were not original, but imported from abroad; and following this lead, I was taken to Eighteenth Century France and thence to England and back to France. I have put more emphasis on France than on England, partly because it seems to have had more influence, and partly because Voltaire, Montesquieu, Rousseau and Turgot interest me more than the English writers. From this I received a clearer idea of the meaning of liberty and equality, and the essential opposition of the two. This contradiction explains many of our present dilemmas. In a program of compromise lies our only hope.

I have tried to bring together in small space several five-foot shelves of books, and to make plain certain old ideas that some people mistake for new. It may be better for our people to recall what was once common sense than to follow certain so-called frontier theories that were tried out long ago and found wanting.

It is a pleasant hobby to study the Fathers of our Country and the Eighteenth Century Philosophers, not only for their sense but for their style. Franklin and Madison, Voltaire and Montesquieu, Rousseau and Condorcet had the ability to express profound ideas in plain language with a wealth of illustration. I wish that I could do the same.

I wish to express my thanks to The Atlantic Monthly, The Teachers College Record, The Journal of Adult Education, and The Proceedings of the National Education Association for permitting me to use parts of articles previously published.

WILLIAM F. RUSSELL

Teachers College
Columbia University
New York City

CONTENTS

		PAGE
I.	So Conceived and So Dedicated	3
II.	Liberté, Égalité	23
III.	Free and Equal	55
IV.	Liberty, Equality and the Power Age	79
V.	Liberty and Learning	97
VI.	Laissez-Faire and Education	119
VII.	Idleness—A Problem and an Opportunity	135
VIII.	Liberty, Equality and National Education	151
IX.	The World of Thought	171

I

SO CONCEIVED AND SO DEDICATED

"Four score and seven years ago our fathers brought forth on this continent, a new nation, conceived in Liberty, and dedicated to the proposition that all men are created equal. Now we are engaged in a great civil war, testing whether that nation, or any nation so conceived and so dedicated, can long endure."

ABRAHAM LINCOLN: *The Gettysburg Address*

"Bearing these explanations in mind, I may now observe that the democratic motto (i.e. Liberty, Equality, Fraternity) involves a contradiction. If human experience proves anything at all, it proves that, if restraints are minimized, if the largest possible measure of liberty is accorded to all human beings, the result will not be equality, but inequality reproducing itself in a geometrical ratio."—JAMES FITZJAMES STEPHEN: *Liberty, Equality, Fraternity,* London 1874, pp. 197–8.

"The formula in which these two terms stand side by side is so dear to the Frenchman who looks back to the Revolution as the date of his emancipation, that perhaps it will be given to others than Frenchmen to see most clearly how complete is the contradiction between liberty and economic equality. . . ."—NICHOLAS MURRAY BUTLER: *True and False Democracy,* March 23, 1907.

I

SO CONCEIVED AND SO DEDICATED

In a recent publication [1] Mr. Hoover states that the American people are faced by the "issue of human liberty." "The whole philosophy of individual liberty is under attack. In haste to bring under control the sweeping social forces unleashed by the political and economic dislocations of the World War, by the tremendous advances in productive technology during the last quarter-century, by the failure to march with a growing sense of justice, peoples and governments are blindly wounding, even destroying, those fundamental human liberties which have been the foundation and inspiration of progress since the Middle Ages." "Men and women have died . . . that the human spirit may be thus free . . . at Plymouth Rock, at Lexington, at Valley Forge, at Yorktown, at New Orleans, at every step of the Western frontier, at Gettysburg, at San Juan Hill, in the Argonne."

According to Mr. Hoover, liberty is freedom

[1] Hoover, Herbert, *The Challenge to Liberty*, Scribners, N. Y., 1934.

LIBERTY vs. EQUALITY

...ip, to think, to hold opinions, to speak
...t fear, to choose one's own calling, to de-
... one's talents, to win and keep a home sacred
... intrusion, to rear children in ordered security,
...arn, to spend, to save and accumulate property
...nestly.

This is an expression of a social faith and today "voices of discouragement join with the voices of other social faiths to assert that an irreconcilable conflict has arisen in which Liberty must be sacrificed upon the altar of the Machine Age." "Once again the United States of America faces the test whether 'a nation so conceived and so dedicated can long endure.'" In subsequent public addresses, Mr. Hoover has stated that recent governmental measures have gone so far toward national regimentation, that they violate the liberties of the American people, and hence are in conflict with the American tradition.

But Mr. Hoover is not the only critic of the New Deal. There are cannon to the right and cannon to the left, and they volley and thunder. Some view the present through red colored spectacles, and some through blue, and the administration turns the other cheek. The New Deal is too radical. The New Deal is too conservative. It has gone too far. It has not gone far enough. In the club car, in the locker room, and at the nineteenth hole there is one opinion. Over the dinner pail there is another. To one group, President Roosevelt is almost a communist; to the other the epitome of capitalism.

To illustrate the opposition of the left wing, I turn to the publications of a movement known as New America. The origin is given as Chicago. I know nothing of the organization, save that some of its directors are members of the Continental Committee on Technocracy. It has a Youth Section. Many of its statements resemble those of certain professors that I know. In its publications it has adopted the pamphleteering technique used by the Jacobin Clubs during the French Revolution.

At the start, this school of thought agrees with Mr. Hoover. "The American nation now stands facing the greatest crisis in its history." But there the similarity ceases. "Have you lost your job?" New America asks. "Is your child through high school, through college, and now can't get a job, or a decent kind of a job? Have you lost your savings? Has your mortgage been foreclosed? The economic machine has broken down. Millions have been deprived of security . . . they are losing their savings, their homes, their farms, the opportunity to educate their children." "We stand," they say, "confused and baffled . . . between disastrous economic and social breakdown on the one hand, and unheard of economic and social possibilities on the other." The American people have had "their heritage taken away from them," and they are now being "denied their future" by the profit system, which we are urged to destroy and to inaugurate in its stead a new social order. "The change must be adequately prepared for, but it must be speedy and thorough." The goals, like those of Technocracy, are (1) "to adjust production to measured consumption requirements," (2) "to eliminate private ownership—(making) profit, rent and interest both unnecessary and impossible," (3) "to reduce the time and energy spent in necessary economic pursuit to a minimum," and (4) "to end unemployment and crises; abolish poverty; enable maximum prevention of crime and disease, and stimulate the arts and sciences." "New America stands for the continuous development of the social order in which there shall be no class divisions or distinctions and no discriminations on account of race or sex; in which able-bodied persons participate in some necessary function of society; in which the principle of maximum and minimum income obtains." "New America springs from American needs,—continues the American Revolutionary tradition and plans to realize the American dream of equalitarian social democracy."

To Mr. Hoover the philosophy of "National Regimentation" is the very negation of American liberalism. To New America, unless "the profit system . . . be replaced with a planned and democratically controlled social economy," we shall not have realized the American Dream. Mr. Hoover would "recall our American heritage"; New America, by drawing the "plans and blueprints of the new society" would restore the "ideals which are our American heritage." [2]

Here we find repeated reference to the same ideals, and at the same time plans for realizing them which are as far apart as the poles. Here we are confronted with diametrically opposed social philosophies which nevertheless appeal to the same justification in history. Is it simply oratory? Are both sides merely waving the flag? Surely we could not accuse Mr. Hoover of a false interpretation of American history; nor am I convinced that the New America pamphlets are written by ignorant men. Can it be possible that both are right?

If one were to ask the thinking American for the ideals of his country, the reply would include such expressions as "life, liberty and the pursuit of happiness," "give me liberty or give me death," "our liberties we prize and our rights we will maintain," "no taxation without representation," "all men are created free and equal," and "all

[2] It is interesting to note that the late Hon. Huey Long, Senator from Louisiana, in his radio address on the night of March 7, 1935 justified his share-the-wealth idea by reference not only to the Mayflower Compact, but also to Daniel Webster, Ralph Waldo Emerson, Abraham Lincoln, Andrew Jackson, William Jennings Bryan and Theodore Roosevelt. As will be noted later, he might have included Diderot, Rousseau, Holbach and Helvétius.

LIBERTY vs. EQUALITY

nments derive their just powers from the
nt of the governed." Lincoln summed up
can ideals when he said, "Four score and
seven years ago our fathers brought forth on this
continent, a new nation, conceived in Liberty,
and dedicated to the proposition that all men
are created equal." Could liberty and equality
as ideals require such diverse means for their
realization? To examine this possibility we shall
follow the history and relation of the two ideals.

We shall begin with the ideal of liberty among
the ancients. We shall follow the progress toward political liberty, the development of freedom of worship, thought, and speech; and the
gradual realization of the possibility of liberating the powers of man from superstition, disease, and ignorance through the work of Francis
Bacon, Locke, Voltaire, Montesquieu, and Diderot. We shall trace the extension of the idea of
liberty to industry, agriculture, and commerce
by following the Physiocrats, Quesnay and Turgot, and later on Adam Smith who developed
the idea of *laissez-faire*. These ideas were brought
to America by some of the first settlers, who
wanted liberty for themselves but not for others;
and were sponsored in their broader conception
by Benjamin Franklin, Thomas Paine, John
Adams and many more. It is interesting to trace
the influence of English and French thought
upon Washington, Hamilton and De Witt Clinton,

upon Madison, John Marshall and Monroe. "Sweet land of liberty" was no accident. The "land of the brave and the free" did not "just grow." It was the culmination of the aspiration and the sacrifice of many generations.

Similarly, the ideal of equality has its roots deep in the past. There is the camel and the needle's eye. Consider the account of the Peasants' Revolt in England in 1381 and the following extract from a sermon which Froissart[3] attributed to John Ball: "A ye good people, the maters gothe nat well to passe in Englande, nor shall nat do tyll euery thyng be comon; and that there be no villayns nor gentylmen, but that we may be all vnyed toguyder, and that the lordes be no greatter maisters than we be. What haue we deserued, or why shulde we be kept thus in seruage? we be all come fro one father and one mother, Adam and Eue; wherby can they say or shewe that they be gretter lordes than we be? sauynge by that they cause vs to wyn and labour, for that they dispende; they ar clothed in veluet and chamlet furred with grise, and we be vestured with pore clothe; they haue their wynes, spyces and good breed, and we haue the drawyng out of the chaffe, and drinke water; they dwell in fayre houses, and we haue the payne and traueyle, rayne, and wynde in the feldes; and by

[3] Lord Berners' *Froissart*, ed. 1812, cap. ccclxxxi, vol. I, pp. 640–641.

that that cometh of our labours they kepe and maynteyne their estates." John Ball, Wat Tyler and Jack Straw gave their lives for equality, but the ideal went marching on. Sometimes it flamed into open revolt. More often it smoldered behind closed doors. John Locke gave it a great advance, when he announced not only that the mind at birth was an empty tablet, but that in consequence all distinctions and discriminations were the result of what went on in the world. Men were unequal only because men themselves made them so. This was taken up by Helvétius and Holbach and by that most eloquent moulder of public opinion, Jean Jacques Rosseau. At the time when, in Europe, equality had so many champions, in America it had a home only on the frontier, and in the minds of a few leaders like Thomas Jefferson. Certainly it was not welcome among the planters of the South, the patroons, nor among the holders of patents from the King.

Liberty and equality sound well together. *Liberté* and *Égalité* grace as an inscription many buildings in France. Lincoln coupled the two ideas in the Gettysburg Address. But they have never liked each other. Liberty and equality have always been locked in a struggle of life and death. Voltaire was caustic in his comments on Helvétius and Rousseau. Turgot ridiculed Holbach's ideas. Hamilton, the exponent of liberty, and Jefferson, the advocate of equality, fought all their lives.

The French Revolution admirably illustrates the conflict. The National Assembly, first in control of the liberals, the advocates of liberty, men like Mirabeau, drafted the Declaration of the Rights of Man, to guarantee freedom of the person, freedom of worship, freedom of speech, and freedom of the press; and it tried to liberate commerce and industry, by legislating the government out of business. Then came the National Convention and Marat and Robespierre with their passion for equality, which not only put the government back, but even guillotined the wealthy. "The deepest cause which made the French Revolution so disastrous to liberty," says Lord Acton, "was its theory of equality."

The struggle between liberty and equality is equally apparent in our own history. Equality loomed large in 1776 and stood first in the Declaration of Independence. By 1787 it had waned, Jefferson was in France, and liberty was supreme in the Constitutional Convention. The Federalist Papers, written by Hamilton, Jay and Madison, in justifying the proposed constitution to the people, made not a single reference to equality.

If we were to paint the canvas with broad swift strokes, I should say that the equalitarians drafted the Declaration of Independence, and the Ordinance of 1785; the liberals drafted the Constitution, and held the power until the time of Andrew Jackson; the liberals founded the colleges and fostered the local control of schools. But it was the equalitarians who built up school funds, demanded state departments of education, and developed our system of public schools. It was working men's societies and fraternal organizations who formed the support of Horace Mann, Gideon Hawley and Henry Barnard.

We have always had organizations in the United States that preferred equality to liberty. There have been Coxey's Armies, I.W.W.'s, Nonpartisan Leagues, and Single Taxers. They say with New America, "Why must millions go undernourished and underclad? Why must 90% of farm homes, 80% of those in villages and 35% in towns be without sanitary plumbing? Why must millions be deprived of the sports, the travel, the scientific knowledge which the few now enjoy?" The Technocrats, the latest group of equalitarians say that they can save our society. We can give everybody equal treatment, they say. We shall provide everybody, not with a happy hunting ground, not with forty acres and a mule, but with everything that $20,000 a year will buy. We shall need to develop a planned economy. We shall organize the entire social and industrial life of the nation, from the Panama Canal to Hudson Bay. By techniques that we have mastered we shall measure the capacity for consumption of the American people and we

SO CONCEIVED AND SO DEDICATED 13

shall plan production to match. We shall keep the machinery of production running evenly to provide all that can be consumed. When necessary, we shall adjust. We shall tell the people what work they are to do, and provide everybody with everything that it is good for them to have. All this can be done, say the Technocrats, by adults from 21 to 45 working a few hours a day for a few days a week. There will be no depressions, no money, no prices, no debts, no taxes, no bankers, no lawyers, no insurance, and neither poor relief nor charity.

And there will be no liberty, either, say the liberals. This is the social order they are trying to establish in Russia, in Italy, and in Germany. The Frontier Thinkers, the Technocrats, the Communists, and the followers of Huey Long can talk all they like about democratic control. It will not work that way. Even the slight efforts in this direction under the New Deal show that orders go with control. True, it may bring a little more equality, but, "Give me liberty or give me death."

So to come back to our original argument. When Mr. Hoover refers to America as a "nation so conceived and so dedicated," he is thinking more of "conceived in liberty" than of "dedicated to equality." New America, in referring to American ideals, is thinking more of equality than of liberty. Freedom, in fact, is dismissed with a few generalities. Nevertheless, both are in the American tradition.

The trouble is that the American Dream is double, and liberty and equality harmonize only in speech. The words look well together, but the ideas behind the words have always been in conflict. If you have liberty to the full, you cannot have equality. If you have equality to the full, you cannot have liberty. If you have more liberty, you will have less equality. If you have more equality, you will have less liberty;—and America, up to now has adopted the policy of the middle course. We say we want just as much liberty as we can have with some equality; or just as much equality as we can have with some liberty. During some periods the pendulum swung toward liberty; at others toward equality. Never was the trend toward liberty strong enough to satisfy a Hamilton. Never was the trend toward equality powerful enough to satisfy an Upton Sinclair. We pursued a middle course.

And in this case, a middle course, a synthesis, a compromise if you will, is the *Strong Position*. We have seen extremists in either direction bring destruction in their wake. For men are so constituted that they want both liberty and equality; and they cannot eat their cake and have it too. Hence, half a loaf is better than no bread.

So the political scientist in the United States has no set pattern to follow. We cannot aim clearly at either extreme. We want as much liberty as we can get, but only so much as will be possible with the equality we want. This will demand the delicate sense of balance of the artist or philosopher. It will require a process of feel and fumble, or trial and error, or adjustment and readjustment, and gradual approximation. It is a tune we shall have to play by ear. This is what we have done for one hundred and fifty years. It is the only road to success.

It seems to be more difficult to find the middle course, to reach the compromise, as we progress from year to year. At the foundation of the nation, as we shall show, the two ideas were not very far apart. The balance was greatly disturbed by the Industrial Revolution; and today, the coming of the Power Age, with its quantity production through technology, has strained the relationship which was working fairly well. The obvious distress of millions of unemployed has raised the question of equality. The increase of government interference in and regulation of supposedly private affairs has raised the question of liberty. The gap between the extremes is becoming wider. Now, more than ever before, is there need of the middle course. Certainly at this time, we should explore every avenue of compromise.

The chief possibility of compromise lies in education;—in our schools, churches, newspapers, theaters, books, journals, radios;—in fact in every agency that helps to form the young. There is nothing new in this idea. The liberals believed that liberty could be achieved only by a widespread system of popular education. Such a system was advocated in Diderot's Encyclopedia. Turgot worked for it. Mirabeau and Lakanal each proposed plans for universal education. Condorcet drafted the plan, including one for adult education, upon which the present system of France is based. Similarly the equalitarians rested their hopes upon education. Rousseau's *Émile*, the culmination of his philosophy, has influenced all education since his day; Holbach and Helvétius stated that equality could be achieved only through education, each wrote upon the subject at length; and Robespierre and Barère submitted long reports upon the subject in the National Convention. Here at least liberals and equalitarians were in agreement.

Just the same agreement was found in the United States. John Adams and James Madison, both liberals, advocated all measures for general education; and so did the equalitarians, such as Thomas Paine. Even Hamilton and Jefferson agreed.

Futhermore the compromises between liberty and equality which were adopted by our fathers, were based largely upon education. We tried to use general education rather than police power

SO CONCEIVED AND SO DEDICATED 17

and government control to prevent turbulence and disrespect for law. Through our school systems, to an increasing degree from year to year, we offered equality of opportunity as a substitute for economic equality, although to many this seems an impossibility. These compromises appear to be breaking under the strain of the depression. Some say they are permanently broken.

Therefore, if it is generally agreed that liberty can be attained largely through popular education, and that equality can be attained largely through popular education; and furthermore if previous compromises between the two have been attained largely through education; may it not be possible that satisfactory compromises between the two may yet be effected by education, even in the difficult days of the future?

This is the possibility that we seek to explore.

For in the search for social justice and the good life, the social ideals of liberty and equality must both be considered and both have a part. If John Ball, or Jean Jacques Rousseau or Karl Marx or other advocates of equality had had full power, it is possible that we should have had bath tubs in more of the remaining 90% of farm homes, 80% of village homes and 35% of town homes; but we should probably have had orders from Washington as to when to take the baths. If Voltaire, or Mirabeau, or Hamilton, or John Adams had had full sway, we should probably have had lords, dukes, and barons, college preparatory schools for the few, and the rest of the pupils in the C.C.C. Camps. It required a constant conflict of the two to reach the golden mean.

This is not the first time that men and women thought that the world was entering upon a new civilization. It has happened over and over again. There are two kinds of waves on the ocean,—the small waves that we see and the great waves, the results of which are the tides. The period since the World War is a small wave. The period from John Locke and Voltaire to the present is a great wave, and we must not confuse the small with the great. During this period of time, in the United States, in parts of Europe, and in some measure elsewhere, men have been trying to achieve the ideals of liberty and equality. The leaders in this movement are not only John Dewey, but also John Ball and John Locke. Not only Tugwell, but also Turgot; Montesquieu and Moley; Counts and Condorcet. Some of these leaders were opposed by kings and princes. Others are being opposed by merchant kings and merchant princes. Some spent years in prison, but their ideas winged free.

Our safety in the United States and the progress of our people toward a happy life, depend upon the degree to which we can effect a compromise between our desires. No philosopher is going to think it through to our satisfaction. No political scientist will suit us with a plan. Our only hope is full, free, frank, open discussion from all sides, open propaganda, open influence upon the press, upon public opinion, upon our congress and legislators, and upon our governors and president. Whoever thinks, let him speak. Whoever would muzzle another, let him stay his hand. Bring on the opposition. Let it be heard. Then shall we have all the forces in full play. Where we have too much liberty and too little equality, we can readjust. Where we have too much equality and too little liberty, we can modify. There may be areas where we have neither. Then we can abolish and create. The political scientist may find compromises in government. The economist may find the middle course in business life. Certainly the educational historian finds that equalitarians and liberals have agreed upon education in the past, and have used it to an increasing degree to bring a measure both of equality and liberty as the conflict between the ideals has deepened. Let us search for every possibility of compromise. Let every possible suggestion be freely made. Let the whole orchestra sound forth. Then in time we can hope that this nation, "conceived in liberty and dedicated to the proposition that all men are created equal," may begin to achieve here on earth that happy combination of the opposing ideals that will yield the best of each,—and at long last reach the goal for which our ancestors have sacrificed and struggled and prayed these many years.

II

LIBERTÉ ÉGALITÉ

"It is true that in democracies the people seem to act as they please; but political liberty does not consist in unlimited freedom. In governments, that is, in societies directed by laws, liberty can consist only in the power of doing what we ought to will, and in not being constrained to do what we ought not to will . . . Liberty is a right of doing whatever the laws permit."
                        MONTESQUIEU, *L'Esprit des Lois*, I.

"The net profit of a society, if equally distributed, may be preferable to a larger profit, if it be unequally distributed and have the effect of dividing the people into two classes, one gorged with riches, the other perishing in misery."
                        DIDEROT, *L'Encyclopédie*.

"Most countries, therefore, must be peopled by the unfortunate. What shall be done to make them happy? Diminish the riches of some; augment that of others; put the poor in such a state of ease that they may by seven or eight hours labor abundantly provide for the wants of themselves and their families. It is then that a people will become as happy as can be."
                        HELVÉTIUS, *De l'Esprit*, pp. 206–7.

"La poule au pot pour tout le monde"—[1]
                        CAMILLE DESMOULINS—

[1] In his address, *Fragment de l'Histoire Secrete de la Révolution,* delivered before the "Friends of Liberty and Equality" on May 19, 1793, Camille Desmoulins stated that this false promise of the kings of France for two hundred years was the ideal of the French Revolution.

II

LIBERTÉ ÉGALITÉ

"We hold these truths to be self-evident," wrote Thomas Jefferson in the Declaration of Independence, ". . . that all men are created equal." "Four score and seven years ago," spoke Abraham Lincoln to the gathering at Gettysburg, "our fathers brought forth on this continent, a new nation, conceived in Liberty, and dedicated to the proposition that all men are created equal." Why did the world wait until 1776 for a nation to dedicate itself to liberty and equality? Surely it was not for want of the desire, for deep down in every heart lies the love for something very close to these ideals.

Suppose we were to spend an evening in a little village in the Balkans. Homeward from the fields we should see the peasants return, upward from the chimneys would rise the smoke of the evening meal, out upon the street would go the promenaders, walking to and fro and gathering in circles to listen to the tellers of tales. We should see the same in China. Down the sunken roads would come the coolies. The old woman and the little girl would cease their round upon the old stone mill. Now within the wattle fences are penned the beasts of the field. The handful of leaves and twigs warms the rice and millet. And after supper, in a ring on the bare earth, sit the men of the village to listen to the teller of tales. It is just the same in New York. Here we jam homewards on the subway or elevated, dine at the delicatessen or automat; and as evening draws on, down the street we go to the "talkies," to see and hear the Hollywood teller of tales. All over the world, after the toil of the day is done, men and women leave the world of hard reality and enter the story world, the land of their hearts' desire. They leave behind the worry and care, the misery and injustice of the world as it is, and for a brief time they live in the world as they would have it be.

What is this world? It is a world where the two older and ugly sisters have gone to the ball leaving poor Cinderella at home. It is a world where, before the evening is done, the fairy prince arrives in his coach and four, fits the golden slipper and bears off his bride. It is a world where the poor little ugly duckling becomes a swan, where Ali Baba finds the treasure of the Forty Thieves, where Aladdin rubs his lamp. When man constructs the kind of a world he wants, it is a world where the weak become strong, the ill well, the feeble powerful and the poor rich.

This same characteristic of man is also shown

by the heroes he venerates. It seems that our delight in recalling greatness in the past increases in proportion to the lowliness of origin. Thus we take great joy in contrasting the mighty law giver with the foundling in the bulrushes, the prophet of Islam with the camel driver, the victor of Austerlitz with the little corporal. The greatest tomb in China venerates the first of the Mings, once a humble Tibetan monk. Why is it that American youths are captivated by the thought of Benjamin Franklin once walking down the street of Philadelphia with a roll under one arm and munching another; or by thoughts of Abraham Lincoln once splitting rails; while George Washington, "first in war, first in peace, first in the hearts of his countrymen," makes no such appeal? Possibly it was because George Washington set out for the West on horseback.

The same characteristic is shown by the tremendous interest in gambling and lotteries. A distinguished citizen once told me that he thought that the people of Porto Rico had never been truly happy since the American occupation because of the abolition of lotteries. Formerly tickets were sold on all sides, and at intervals when the drawings were made, some poor farmer, laborer or teacher, might awake to find himself independent. The results of the Derby or the Grand National make front page news all over the world, not because of interest in the horse, the jockey, the owner or even the contest itself, but for the results of the sweepstakes which depend upon it. The newspapers stress the story of the winners of the lottery. As I write France is all agog because thirty seamstresses in one house in Paris have just won the *grand lot* of 3,000,000 francs. The road may be hot and dusty, the toil wearying and long, but another race will be run, another drawing will be made, and perhaps fortune may light upon me. Napoleon stated that every soldier of France carried in his knapsack the baton of a marshal. A statistician, knowing the number of soldiers and the number of marshals could determine the fractional part of a baton which each soldier carried. Certainly it would be so small as to be invisible, and so slight as to be imperceptible; yet this minute atom made light the load, made straight the road and inflamed the courage. Doctors say, "While there's life, there's hope." It is just as true to say, "While there's hope, there's life."

So, the universality of the appeal of the Cinderella story, the joy in recalling the great of humble origin, and the delight in the results of the lottery, either in participation or contemplation, give justification to the statement that deep down within us, there is a delight, almost as fundamental as food when we are hungry, and drink when we are thirsty, in helping the poor, in educating the ignorant, in advancing the humble, in righting wrongs. Men like to see good fortune come to those who deserve it. This is the beginning of the ideal of equality.

In a similar way, all men love liberty. Few people see an eagle in a cage or a lion in the zoo without an impulse to turn them free. Even the desperate criminal awakens a chord of sympathy. Man wants to be free, to be beyond bounds, to arise when he pleases, to do as he chooses, to follow no orders, to live to himself alone,—and to his family. He wants liberty to think as he likes, to hold what beliefs he chooses, and to speak his mind.

In simple terms these are the ideals of liberty and equality as they are found deep in the nature of man. Equality is the desire to see every person enjoy the health, education, power, position and wealth that the few enjoy. Liberty is the hope that man, each man, every man, may do as he pleases.

But it is idle to try to define liberty and equality positively, for in the development of these ideals, we rarely find a positive statement of either. The love of equality is usually expressed as a hatred of inequality. Witness protests against the excesses and extravagances of the rich; against the poverty, misery and unhappy plight of the poor; against the arrogance of the educated; against the helplessness of the ignorant; against the deafness of the favored few to the pleas of the great mass of mankind. Thomas Jefferson expressed his love of liberty by stating, "I have sworn upon the altar of God, eternal hostility against every form of tyranny over the mind of man."

For never, at any time have men had very much of either liberty or equality. Liberty they have had to sacrifice to security, and equality to the impossibility of the wide distribution of the good things of life when there was so little to go around.

It was not long ago that I had occasion to visit the ancient citadel of Les Baux. We turned south from the high road from Tarascon to Aix-en-Provence, drove into the hill country, and finally took a small side road leading up a mountain side. High above us, perched on the top of a hill, we soon saw the snowy limestone cliffs. More and more slowly pounded our automobile, nearer and nearer to the boiling point rose the thermometer on the radiator, in second speed, and then in low, we made the grade that had been traversed through the centuries. For on top was a small modern village, a fifteenth century castle, the remains of an eleventh century castle, caves with Visigothic remains, Roman work, Greek, Phoenician; and in one cave an archæologist was sifting from the dust of the floor crude stone and bone implements of prehistoric man. The fields down below the hill were broad and fertile, the country was beautiful to look upon, yet from time immemorial men and women had toiled up that hill to pen themselves behind closed walls. We can see the same thing in many places in Europe, at Eze and St. Flour, at Edinburgh and Sterling, at Ravello and Orvieto. Man wants to be free, but what is the use when a pirate may descend upon you, steal your goods, enslave your family and kill yourself. Of course, you would prefer to trudge up the hill and beg the lord of the castle to let you live there. You would be glad to do what he told you to do. You would trade your liberty for some measure of security. A man would rather be a live dog than a dead lion. At least he would for a while.

But while we love liberty for ourselves, unfortunately we have a strong distrust of liberty for anyone else. Arrogance grows apace, and once in a position of power, it is easy for a man to become increasingly unjust. So men who have traded their liberty for security have found themselves abused,—and they or their children have tried to regain their freedom. Up the hill they have climbed to get security, and down the hill they have stolen, saying "Give me liberty or give me death." There have been Robin Hoods and Pilgrim Fathers throughout the ages. Liberty seemed impossible to achieve.

Similarly there was little hope for equality. It is true that there had been essential equality among those who had nothing, like primitive tribes; or among those who wanted practically nothing, like the Spartans. But in the course of history as trade began to increase, man's fortune to grow and cities to develop, the few began to live at the expense of the many.

Once upon a time, when I was walking down a street in Shanghai, I noticed that apparently every store in sight sold nothing but lottery tickets. I asked a Chinese friend, "Isn't this a tremendous social waste?" "I am not so sure," was the reply. "Suppose that there are fifty men each with only the slightest amount of money over and above his minimum needs. Suppose that each can afford one dollar a year and not starve. Suppose that an overcoat costs fifty dollars. Isn't it better for one to be warm and forty-nine cold, than for all fifty to go without an overcoat?"

This was the opinion that used to be held regarding the problem of equality. There never was enough to go around. If you took from the rich and fortunate everything that they had, and divided it among all, everybody would be poor, and none better off.

So constant warfare and an absence of law and order made liberty give way to security; and an economy of scarcity made equality nothing more than a dream.

But even if there had been peace and plenty, there would have been neither liberty nor equality, because the mind of man used to be bur-

LIBERTÉ ÉGALITÉ

dened with the idea of *fatality*. It is very difficult for us today to understand this. We assume that the world is getting better, that our scientists, technologists and philosophers will in time solve the perplexing difficulties of this world; and if we but use our intelligence we shall in time control our environment and ourselves. Our ancestors had no such idea at all. They believed that the golden age lay in the remote past, and that year after year conditions were becoming worse. Unfortunately there was nothing that one could do about it. Everything, man and beast, field and crop, stick and stone, lay in the grip of an inexorable power that moved as it pleased. Man could dream; he could hope; he could beg; but he was helpless. To our ancestors the world looked just the way my game of golf looks to me. My drive starts with the best will in the world; but then in a beautiful curve, the ball slices into the rough. I think I can locate the trouble. It is a matter of stance, grip, left arm, backswing, pivot, follow through and eye. I practice, I study, I strive, but the ball still curves to the right. All I can do is to call upon some supernatural power. This is the way our ancestors looked upon the world. A schoolmaster can understand this outlook upon life. Always in the back row of a class is some football player whose blood is serving muscle and brawn to the exclusion of neurones. We can assign a lesson. Everyone else knows it. What to do? We question, explain, point out, illustrate and diagram. No result. We give special instruction after school. Nothing happens. All that we do is without result. All efforts are in vain. This is the way men used to look upon the world. It is the *idea of fatality,* as contrasted with the *idea of progress.* You might love liberty, but what was the use. You might long for equality, but why oppose the fates.

Christianity had solved the problem of liberty and equality. There was a world where all men would be free; there was a world where all men would be brothers, and have equality. But it was not this world,—it was the Future Life. The power to enter lay in the hands of every man, even the humblest. No prince or potentate had a place more favorable than that of the poorest slave. In the future life, expressed in all forms of allegory, there was to be a happy state, where the fondest desires of man would be realized. It would be easier for a camel to go through the eye of a needle than for a rich man to enter. All that was needed was a love of God and a love of man, expressed in faith and works. One was asked to attend to the future world and to disregard the injustices of this. This does not mean that the Christian church ignored this world. Far from it. It taught liberty and equality. But the *idea of fatality* persisted.

But then, about the time of the Renaissance

LIBERTÉ ÉGALITÉ

something happened in the world. A few thinkers, here and there, began to inquire into the nature of man and the world around him. In this monastery, in that castle, in this university or that academy, a newly found ancient manuscript started thought, a crude experiment yielded a new idea. Men began to explore and to come into contact with strange civilizations. Manuscripts were passed from hand to hand. Printing was discovered and ideas, once held by a few, began to circulate freely.

Many men began to inquire into what we now call science, into the human body and the animal, into the heavens and the microscopic world, into plants and birds and fish, into stones and chemicals, into light and heat. Lord Bacon gathered these materials together and published the first part of a compendium of all human knowledge. He planned to organize into one vast work all that man knew. He saw the world of the future, not in the grip of some obscure fatalistic power, but in the grip of man. Man, he thought, has within himself the power to control all he surveys. In the *New Atlantis* Bacon describes the world as he thinks it might become, a world where men are free, a world where all share the good things of life, a world where the scientist is supreme. For Bacon the golden age lies ahead, not behind; nor need one await the beneficent action of some kind providence. What we need to do is to get to work—to inquire, to compare, to experiment, to test; and in time we shall be able to control the world and ourselves.

There were also men, here and there and everywhere, who began again to inquire into man himself. Why was he on earth? What was his purpose? How did he develop? How did he know good and bad and the difference between them? Was he free? or directed? How did he feel or think or enjoy? Contributions were made by myriads of philosophers, known and unknown, until John Locke brought many of these ideas together and wrote his *Essay on the Human Understanding*. This work has had a most powerful effect on the efforts of the last two hundred years.

For John Locke made the keystone of his work the idea that at birth the soul of man was a *tabula rasa,* an empty tablet; and that everything that followed, all that he developed into, was the result of what went on around him. His speech, his ideas, his conscience, his sensibilities were the result of happenings in this world. ". . . I think I may say," says Locke, "that, of all the men we meet with, nine parts of ten are what they are, good or evil, useful or not, by their education. It is that which makes the great difference in mankind. The little or almost insensible impressions on our tender infancies, have very important and lasting consequences: and there it is, as in the fountains of some rivers, where a gentle application of the hand turns the flexible waters into channels, that make them take quite contrary courses; and by this little direction given them at first in the source, they receive different tendencies, and arrive at last at very remote and distant places. I imagine the minds of children as easily turned this or that way, as water itself. . . ." [2]

The discoveries culminating in Bacon and Newton, and stimulated by them and the attitude toward the human mind advanced by Locke and stimulated by him, turned the attention of man to the importance and possibility of improving this world. At last it was realized that man need placate no fatalistic power. To continue Locke's figure, man was not being swept down the river of life, at the mercy of fortuitous currents, striking this rock, being washed up on that shore, helpless in the cruel waves until at last he reached the sea. On the contrary man had within himself the power to breast the current, or divert it. All that was needed was the vision, and through science, the development of mastery over his environment and himself. He could protect himself against disease, he could learn to produce enough to satisfy all his needs and desires, he could develop commerce, industry and government, he could abolish poverty and war. The

[2] Locke, John: *Some Thoughts Concerning Education*, London, 1880, p. 60.

Kingdom of Heaven might come here on earth.

This was the idea of the Eighteenth Century philosophers,—who gave Franklin and Jefferson, Hamilton and Monroe and the other Fathers of our country, their ideas of liberty and equality. All too often we are persuaded to look upon this movement as one that was negative, anti-religious, anti-government, opposed to all that was stable and good. We must remember that church and state, being human institutions, in the control of men, had developed those abuses that men are likely to develop when they have enjoyed too long unchecked an abundance of power. In France, at the beginning of the Eighteenth Century, the heretic and the communist were not popular. Men were imprisoned for criticizing those in power. Few writers dared to sign their writings. Men were thrown into jail for speaking their minds. Taxes were levied at the sweet will of the master. Nobles were privileged to hunt over the fields and to ruin the crops of the peasants without recourse; and the poor could not even kill a pigeon. The price of meat and bread, of cloth and firewood, even the right to transport goods, the right to engage in a trade or occupation,—all were in the hands of state monopolies. The poor man was tied down tight.

The Eighteenth Century philosophers planned to improve this world, and the people accepted their ideas with startling suddenness. Professor

LIBERTÉ ÉGALITÉ

Paul Hazard of the Collège de France has just published a great work [3] in which he traces the change in ideas in Europe from 1680 to 1715. Here is his opening statement:

"What a contrast! What a sudden change. The ideas of the Seventeenth Century were social stratification, discipline, order under authority and a set of beliefs which firmly ruled life. In contrast, their immediate successors, the men of the Eighteenth Century hated all constraint, authority and dogma. The former were Christians, the latter anti-Christian; the former believed in Divine Law, the latter in Natural Law; the former lived at ease in a society divided into classes, the latter yearned only for equality. The new generation took delight in criticizing the older; it imagined that it was about to reform a world that had waited all this time for the arrival of this particular new generation at last to progress. Most of the French used to think like Bossuet; all of a sudden they thought like Voltaire. It was a revolution!"

And how did Voltaire think? He was a brilliant man, combining in his own person the best of his day. He was Bernard Shaw, Eugene O'Neill, John Dewey, Walter Lippmann, and Julian Huxley all rolled into one. He was the best dramatist, essayist, philosopher, critic and re-

[3] Hazard, Paul: *La Crise de la Conscience Européenne.* 1680–1715, Paris, 1935.

porter on the progress of science of his day. He became a wealthy man. His people rendered him honors beyond that of any king. He is thought of as an opponent of religion. More truly he was an opponent of all tyranny,—an advocate of liberty in every form.

"To be secure on lying down," he wrote, "that you shall rise in possession of the same property with which you retired to rest, that you shall not be torn from the arms of your wife, and from your children, in the dead of night, to be thrown into a dungeon, or buried in exile in a desert; that, when rising from the bed of sleep, you will have the power of publishing all your thoughts; and that, if you are accused of having either acted, spoken, or written wrongly, you can be tried only according to law. These privileges attach to every one who set foot on English ground . . . I will venture to assert, that, were the human race solemnly assembled for the purpose of making laws, such are the laws they would make for their security."[4]

Men read Voltaire. They caught the idea of a natural explanation of the supernatural, of a reasonable explanation of most of the problems of life; and along with Voltaire they decided to attack the strongholds of tyranny. They said to themselves, the world does not have to con-

[4] The Works of Voltaire, New York, 1901 (John Morley), Vol. V, Pt. 1, p. 294.

LIBERTÉ ÉGALITÉ

tinue as it is. Liberty is not beyond our grasp. If we like, we can have a government of free men, religious liberty, freedom of thought, freedom of speech and freedom of the press. If affairs continue as they are, we have no one but ourselves to blame.

Montesquieu, another great philosopher, turned his searchlight on government. He looked into the past and all round about him in search of an answer to the question, "How have men governed themselves and what are the best kinds of government?" To Montesquieu government was no mysterious, unchangeable institution foisted by supernatural powers upon unwilling men. Government, on the contrary, was man-created and man-developed; and what man has created and developed he can modify and improve. Just as man can learn to grow better wheat and control disease, so he can eradicate a bad government and substitute a better. "This," said John Morley, referring to the contribution of Montesquieu, "was a very marked advance upon both of the ideas, by one or the other of which men had previously been content to explain to themselves the course of circumstances in the world, either the inscrutable decrees of an inhuman providence, or the fortuitous vagaries of an eyeless destiny." In the *Esprit des Lois,* Montesquieu presented to mankind a text book describing a great variety of forms of government, contemporary and in the past, and pointed out their good and bad points and their advantages and disadvantages. He brought to the attention of all the problem of government and the possibility of improvement.

In 1745 Le Breton, an enterprising publisher of Paris, got the idea of publishing a French translation of a recent English work, *Chamber's Encyclopedia;* and by a fortunate chance, approached an impecunious hack-writer, Denis Diderot, by name, to undertake the task. Diderot turned out to be the most brilliant man of the Eighteenth Century. Instead of accepting the task of translating a second-rate English work, he conceived the idea of once and for all accomplishing the task that Bacon had set for himself one hundred and fifty years before. All that the world needs is knowledge. Science is advancing apace. Technical processes are changing all the time. Inventions and discoveries are being made every day. There are the beginnings of a science of politics. The philosophers have worked out solutions to most of the problems of life. As d'Alembert pointed out in the famous preface, the projected work was to be not only an encyclopedia expressing the attitude of the philosophers on all the problems of mankind, but also a dictionary of science bringing together all the facts known to man about life and how to live in this world. Diderot enlisted a brilliant group

LIBERTÉ ÉGALITÉ

of men to work with him, including d'Alembert, Rousseau, Voltaire, Turgot, and many others. The main idea was the improvement of life. Eleven of the twenty-eight volumes are devoted entirely to engravings depicting graphically tools, processes, plants, animals, systems of architecture, building, manufacture, mining, and the like.

The first two volumes appeared in 1751 with the names of Diderot and d'Alembert on the title page, and four Paris firms as publishers. Volumes VIII–XVII, although actually printed in Paris, bore the imprint of Neufchatel, and Diderot and d'Alembert did not dare to sign their names. For the early volumes of the Encyclopedia were fearless. The authors spoke their minds, daring to offend prince and priest. Some of the recent proposals of Huey Long, Upton Sinclair and Father Coughlin are mild in comparison. There was all sorts of trouble. The authors were threatened with imprisonment and banishment. The publishers, fearing the censors, often altered contributions after proof had been read by editors and authors. In many places, one must read between the lines, especially on religious matters. These books were eagerly bought all over France and they were minutely studied in countless homes.

Here was a compendium of information and a great collection of propaganda for new ideas, especially liberty in all its forms. Man had the world in his grasp, and if he but desired he could change it at will. Science could rule the world. Man could have what he wanted, even liberty and equality.

The idea of liberty applied to religion, government, speech and press was carried into the realm of economics by Quesnay, the elder Mirabeau, Dupont de Nemours, Turgot, Condorcet and the other Physiocrats. Following Colbert, and to a great degree throughout history, government dominated all the affairs of agriculture, business, industry and commerce. There were countless minute regulations which were set forth by government orders, and a host of functionaries to enforce them. Such things as the shape of handkerchiefs, the type of boat to be used by the Breton fishermen, and the method of fishing in Languedoc were all prescribed by the government. The Physiocrats conceived the idea that it would be better, if the government were to give complete freedom to all. This new philosophy was expressed concisely by Benjamin Franklin, who knew the Physiocrats and had met with them in Paris.

"Perhaps, in general, it would be better if government meddled no farther with trade, than to protect it and let it take its course. Most of the statutes or acts, edicts, *arrêts* and placarts of parliaments, princes and states, for regulating, directing or restraining of trade, have, we think, been

LIBERTÉ ÉGALITÉ

either political blunders, or jobs obtained by artful men for private advantage under pretense of public good. When Colbert assembled some wise old merchants of France, and desired their advice and opinion, how he could best serve and promote commerce, their answer, after consultation, was in three words only, *laissez-nous faire,* 'Let us alone.' It is said by a very solid writer of the same nation, that he is well advanced in the science of politics, who knows the full force of that maxim, *pas trop gouverner,* 'Not to govern too much.' " [5]

This brief discussion serves to point out only a few of the high spots in the development of the idea of liberty in France during the Eighteenth Century. To give a true picture would require many volumes. Professor Hazard has shown the tremendous change that took place in man's thought from 1680 to 1715. Professor Mornet of the Sorbonne, in his *Les Origines Intellectuelles de la Révolution Française* has traced the development of these ideas during three periods, from 1715 to 1748, from 1748 to 1770 and from 1770 to 1787. He comes to his conclusions after the widest reading, consultation of thousands of original documents, and attention directed quite as much to the provinces as to Paris itself. He depicts the slow and spasmodic development of the ideas up to the middle of the century, and

[5] Works, Vol. II, p. 401.

their rapid acceleration after 1770. Everything that we have attributed to the great was previously expressed by some obscure writer. Opposition to what was preceded advocacy of what should be. Everywhere in all ways were sown the seeds of liberty, and a combination of many forces made them spread and grow. Books were written and pamphlets, journals and newspapers published, reading rooms were established, learned societies, clubs and fraternal organizations took up the cause of liberty, and universities and schools played their part. Like a great wave, all over France, arose a tremendous popular desire for liberty of conscience, liberty before the law, freedom of speech and of the press, and economic liberty, laissez-faire.

So far we have considered the growth of the idea of liberty. At the same time the idea of equality was developing apace. John Locke's notion that at birth the mind of man was an empty tablet, and that most differences among men were caused by what men did, not only gave men the courage to try to effect some reforms in the world, but it also shed new light upon the inequalities existing among men. One man lived in a castle, another in a hovel; one was clothed in fine raiment, another in rags; one had delicacies to eat, the other the poorest of food; and if one follows Locke's idea to its logical conclusion this condition is not caused by

LIBERTÉ ÉGALITÉ

Divine Will, or by fate, but by something that was done by man himself; and what man has done, man can correct.

This point of view was materially aided, as Professor Hazard has pointed out, by a series of books on travel and descriptions of imaginary societies which appeared shortly before and after the beginning of the Eighteenth Century. Baron de Lahontan, for example, after a career of Indian fighting in Canada, returned to France and published his *Voyages, Memoires,* and *Dialogues.* Here was a new idea! America was peopled by *good savages.* These Hurons were happier, wiser and really more civilized than the French. They were ruled by natural law, not man-made; they had established a primitive communism, and were not burdened with private possessions; they were self-reliant and self-sufficient; they sought no false gods. All received justice. All enjoyed liberty and equality, because they followed Mother Nature. In contrast, the so-called civilized peoples were weak, effeminate, helpless, and sick unto death with the ills of civilization.

Many other books were published with the same idea in mind. There were accounts of Persia, Turkey, China, Siam, Africa; and accounts of this imaginary island or that, upon which this mariner or that had been shipwrecked. Of course the idea is mostly false; but the important thing is that the people of France and other countries of Europe began to believe that possibly savages were happier than Europeans and that they certainly enjoyed more equality, and possibly a great deal more liberty. These works paved the way for Rousseau.

In 1750 Rousseau won the prize offered by the Academy of Dijon with an essay in which he showed how man had degenerated under civilization; and in 1755 he published his essay on inequality, in which he describes the origin and development of inequality among men. Rousseau admits at the start that there are inequalities like differences in age, health, strength and intelligence about which nothing can be done. He confines his attention to what he calls *moral* or *political* inequality, which consists of the "privileges which are enjoyed by some at the expense of others, such as being richer, more honored, more powerful, or able to make others obey." He harps on the old theme of the equality among primitive men, and step by step shows how inequality and hence unhappiness grows with civilization. He preaches with the greatest eloquence the possibility of correcting these evils. Rousseau did not believe in exact economic equality. In the *Social Contract* he makes several statements about equality. "Everyone should have something, and none too much." "The ideal state is one in which there are neither rich nor poor." ". . . As for equality, it should not mean that all degrees of power and wealth should be exactly the same; rather it should mean that power should never be gained by force or violence, and it should be exercised in an orderly manner and according to law; and as for wealth, no citizen should be rich enough to be able to buy another, and none so poor as to be forced to sell himself."[6] "If you wish to secure stability in a State, bring the extremes of wealth as close together as possible. Suffer neither wealthy men nor beggars. These two estates, which naturally go together, are equally disastrous to the common good, from the one come the creators of tyranny, from the other the tyrants; and it is these two groups that traffic in popular liberty, the one buys and the other sells."[7] Despotism and inequality result from the violation of the laws of Nature. In the good old days when men were primitive, they were equal and happy. What we need to do is to reëstablish the old order. Rousseau wrote with such simplicity, clarity and power that his message carried far and wide; and men began to believe him.

Helvétius in his two books *De l'Esprit* and *De l'Homme* and Holbach in his *Système de la Nature* came to the same conclusion. These philosophers began where Locke left off. The universe is materialistic. It should be judged and under-

[6] Rousseau, Jean Jacques: *Social Contract,* II, Chap. XI.
[7] *Ibid.,* II, Chap. XI, note.

stood on a materialistic basis. There is nothing in Divine Power. Nothing in fatality. "We do not need," said Holbach, "to go to an ideal world, which exists only in the imagination, to seek the motives which operate in this." If we wish to improve society, we have the power in our hands. "In the moral world just as in the physical, a cause is necessarily followed by its effect. The real reason for the unhappiness and misery of mankind lies in custom and education." Helvétius gives an interesting illustration of his idea of the human mind. "It would seem that we see, or believe we see," he says, "the necessary relations of cause and effect, far more distinctly in physics than in the human mind. There, at least, we admit that certain known causes produce certain known effects, always the same when the circumstances are the same. In the physical world, at least, we do not hesitate to consider physical results as necessary, while we refuse to admit this of the human will. We falsely think that man is a free moving being, capable of acting under his own power, capable of modifying himself without the assistance of external causes; and thus is different from all physical and material things. Agriculture is based upon the assurance, coming from experience, that the soil can be compelled to grow the grain and fruit necessary to our subsistence, when it is cultivated and seeded in a certain way, and has certain other necessary characteristics. If we could only rise above prejudice, we should see in the moral and mental world, that education is nothing but the *agriculture of the spirit,* and that like the soil, because of its natural qualities and the culture which is given it, if seeds are sown, and the seasons are favorable enough to bring them to maturity, we are certain that the soil will produce vices or virtues, i.e., *moral fruits,* helpful or harmful to society." [8]

According to Helvétius and Holbach men are equal when they are born. Whatever happens to them, good or ill, is caused by something in this world, not the next. There need be no mystery about the human mind, the spirit, the will or the soul. They are subject to the laws of nature. Differences among men, morality or immorality, virtue or vice, happiness or misery, are mainly the results of how we bring up our children. If we but use our intelligence, we can do almost what we want with the next generation. Inequalities are the result of bad education. A proper education will bring virtue, liberty, equality, a good government, a happy people and international peace.

Thus in France, and to a considerable degree elsewhere in Europe, the citizens of the Eighteenth Century were bombarded with a host of

[8] Holbach, *Système de la Nature,* Londres, 1770, I, pp. 210–11.

new ideas. It was obvious that there was something wrong with the world. Governments were despotic. Taxation was burdensome and unjust. Treasuries were bankrupt. Courts were vicious and immoral. The clergy was stupid and tyrannical. Business was in the hands of State monopolies. Philosophers and authors languished in prison for what they said and wrote. The poor became poorer and the wealthy flaunted their opulence. Something was wrong. Voltaire had sung the song of liberty. He had successfully championed Calas and other subjects of tyranny. Montesquieu had demonstrated that there were good governments in the world,—and bad,—and that something could be done about it. Diderot, d'Alembert and the Encyclopedists had shown not only that man had the power to improve his life and that science could bring abundance; but that liberty and equality were within his grasp. Turgot and the Physiocrats had shown the value of liberty in agriculture, business, trade and industry. Rousseau had emphasized the ills of civilization by contrasting Europe with the imaginary blessings of savage life; and together with Helvétius and Holbach had exalted the ideal of equality and had demonstrated the tremendous power that man controls in his ability to change and form the mind of the young.

Mankind had dreamed of liberty and equality across the ages. At last it seemed that they might be possible of achievement. The time was not far distant when men were going to act; and it was in a little group of English colonies far across the seas, that they acted first.

III

FREE AND EQUAL

"Give me liberty or give me death."
PATRICK HENRY.

"All men are created equal."
DECLARATION OF INDEPENDENCE.

"One man is as good as another, if not better."
MR. DOOLEY.

III

FREE AND EQUAL

AMERICA grew to love liberty and equality, but there was nothing automatic about this development. The climate of America did not breed liberty, nor did its geography foster equality. Nothing is farther from the truth than the belief that the "fierce spirit of liberty" and "hope of equality" pervaded all the early settlers alike; that all newcomers embraced these ideals; and that then there evolved a process of gentle evolution. It is true that the Pilgrim Fathers came in search of religious liberty for themselves; but they denied this privilege to others. It is also true that the Mayflower Compact went far toward political and even economic equality. But the Pilgrims were only a small group among a large number of colonists.

What happened was simply this. Most of the colonies were settled under grants of the King to favored organizations or individuals. This put a ruling class in power at the start. These large land owners, or organizations, imported colonists, often the poor, the humble and the destitute. These colonists worked for the owners. The rich exploited the poor. Even the colonies, like Plymouth, that started with everybody poor and nearly equal, found that brains, thrift and enterprise soon operated to form distinctions of caste and class. As a colony grew older whatever liberty and equality may have been present at the start tended to diminish; and these ideals would have vanished from the American scene but for the operation of two forces. The first of these was the frontier, which was steadily being extended across the mountains into the West. The seaboard might lie in the clutches of Royal Governors and wealthy land-owners, but on beyond, on the edge of the Indian country, there was a place where men were equal and free; and into these settlements poured those enticed by ideals of liberty and equality or conversely those oppressed by the authorities and destitute of hope.

The second factor, tending to preserve the ideals of liberty and equality, was the presence of radicals, zealots, propagandists, critics of the social order, who had a love for their fellow men and an earnest desire to reform the world. They became familiar with what was going on among the French philosophers. They read Voltaire, Montesquieu and Rousseau, either in the original or in English translation. They had in their libraries the works of the English philosophers who had been influenced by the French.

FREE AND EQUAL

By the middle of the Eighteenth Century there was less liberty and equality in America than there had been a hundred years before. By the democratic communities in the backwoods, and by the radicals on the seaboard, the struggle for liberty and equality was maintained. All this was stimulated by the stupidity of English misrule. From the time of the Albany Convention in 1749, the leading men among the reformers had been speculating upon some plan of union for the colonies; and certainly for a decade before 1776, there had been growing talk of the need of separation from England. We can plainly see, by studying the collected works of Jefferson and Madison, of John Adams and Hamilton, of John Jay and Patrick Henry and Benjamin Franklin how these men patiently took pains to master the best that had been thought and said regarding the welfare and improvement of mankind and the relation of government to it. After Lexington and Concord and Bunker Hill, the Continental Congress drew up formally its Declaration of Independence, which commenced as follows:

"When in the Course of human events, it becomes necessary for one people to dissolve the political bands which have connected them with another, and to assume among the Powers of the earth, the separate and equal station to which the Laws of Nature and of Nature's God entitle them, a decent respect to the opinions of mankind requires that they should declare the causes which impel them to the separation.

"We hold these truths to be self-evident, that all men are created equal, that they are endowed by their Creator with certain unalienable Rights, that among these are Life, Liberty, and the pursuit of Happiness."

Our attention at once centers upon the phraseology and the use of certain strange words. What are the Laws of Nature? What is Nature's God? Why is it self-evident that all men are created equal? Why are life, liberty and the pursuit of happiness inalienable rights with which man is endowed? It is obvious, of course, that these phrases link the signers of the Declaration of Independence with Locke, Voltaire, Montesquieu, Rousseau, Helvétius, Holbach and the Encyclopedists. And it was not idle talk. These colonists were fighting a war against a great power, not merely to free themselves from oppression, but at last, here on earth, to establish a society in which men would be free and equal. "America hoped to become a great nation," says James Truslow Adams. "Every great nation then in the world was monarchical and aristocratical. America began as a republic and had made a long step toward a democracy. That was something radically new, though the political philosophy was not

... What was wholly novel was the putting of the theory into practice."[1]

At the outbreak of the Revolutionary War, the Thirteen Colonies had been forced to set up a central government for the prosecution of the war and the administration of common enterprises. Each colony, now judging itself free, had been forced to adopt a new constitution. But as the war reached a successful conclusion, the binding force of a common peril began to wane, and the weaknesses of the Articles of Confederation became increasingly apparent. The wheels of government creaked and groaned, and at last almost refused to turn. So it was in 1786 that the Annapolis Convention sent out a call for a meeting of representatives of the states to form a new constitution for the country as a whole. Throughout the heat of the Philadelphia summer of 1787 sat another group of men, gathered together to conceive a new nation. Washington presided at every session. Franklin attended, but to judge from Madison's *Journal* did not contribute very much. Hamilton dropped in briefly on two occasions, but had little influence. The lion's share of the work was done by Madison, Pinckney, Gerry, Rutledge and Wilson.

There is not much point in discussing what

[1] Adams, James Truslow: *The Epic of America,* Little, Brown, and Co., Boston, 1934, p. 100.

these men said about liberty. Everyone wanted it. As Voltaire once said, "In all disputes on liberty, one reasoner generally understands one theory, and his adversary another. A third comes in and understands neither one or the other, or is himself understood . . . each revolves in his own circle and they never meet." The idea of liberty of the Fathers of the Republic is best shown by what they did.

In the first place, their ideal of political liberty is shown by the cumbersome government which they created. They could easily have made one that would have been far more efficient, but their ideal was to have one just as effective as possible and at the same time run no danger of becoming tyrannical. As Hamilton said, "Good constitutions are formed upon a comparison of the liberty of the individual with the strength of government. If the tone of either be too high, the other will be weakened too much. It is the happiest possible mode of conciliating these objects, to institute one branch peculiarly endowed with sensibility, another with knowledge and firmness. Through the opposition and mutual control of these bodies, the government will reach, in its operations, the perfect balance between liberty and power." [2] It was to preserve liberty that the plan was devised, following the sug-

[2] Lodge: *The Works of Alexander Hamilton*, N. Y., 1885, I, p. 459.

gestion of Montesquieu, to balance powers between the President, Congress and the Supreme Court. It was to preserve liberty that Congress was divided into a House of Representatives and a Senate. It was to preserve liberty that the locality retained sovereignty over local affairs, and the state over state affairs, while the nation was given very little power indeed. Jefferson expressed the ideal in his First Inaugural Address: ". . . a wise and frugal government, which shall restrain men from injuring one another, shall leave them otherwise free to regulate their own pursuits of industry and improvement, and shall not take from the mouth of labor the bread it has earned. This is the sum of good government and this is necessary to close the circle of our felicities." Whatever power was to be granted by the locality to the state or by the state to the Federal government was to be stated plainly in writing. It was to be a government of law,—not of men.

The ideal of liberty is further shown by the care taken to guard the rights of the individual. The Constitution took pains to safeguard certain individual rights, and it was adopted by the States upon the express stipulation that the first ten amendments should be adopted, thus giving us the Bill of Rights. Treason was specifically defined. The rights of trial by jury, habeas corpus, procedure for trial, arrest and imprisonment, freedom of conscience, of speech and of the press were minutely defined in the Constitution. Furthermore the government was kept out of business. Relatively few powers such as the determination of weights and measures, coinage and transportation of the mails were reserved to the Federal government. This was in accord with the ideas of the Physiocrats and Adam Smith, the exponents of laissez-faire.

The ideal of liberty in the early days of the Republic is further shown by the attitude of the Fathers to the problem of general education. Every protector of liberty believed that while a proper government and a bill of rights would conserve liberty, its real source lay in public opinion and in the minds and attitudes of the people. Nothing is easier than to quote Washington, Hamilton, Adams, Thomas Paine, Jefferson, Franklin, Madison, Marshall and Monroe on the subject of education. "I consider," wrote De Witt Clinton, "the system of our common schools as the palladium of our freedom, for no reasonable apprehension can be entertained of its subversion, as long as the great body of the people are enlightened by education."

Why, then, did the Constitution of the United States say nothing about public education? The answer is that the Framers of the Constitution thought that they had!

According to Madison's *Journal,* on August 6,

FREE AND EQUAL

1787, after the Convention had been in session some two months, a committee under the chairmanship of John Rutledge reported a draft of the proposed Constitution of the United States incorporating the provisions agreed upon up to that time. After ten days of discussion, the Convention reached the section dealing with powers to be conferred upon Congress. Some fifteen powers had previously been voted, such as the powers to lay and collect taxes, to coin money, to subdue rebellions, and to make war. On August 18th, as the discussion appeared to be drawing to a close, Madison rose and moved nine additional powers for Congress and Pinckney suggested eleven others. These twenty suggested powers were referred back to Rutledge's Committee for recommendations. On August 22 the committee made its report. Four of the suggested powers (those having to do with Indians, finances and debts) were dealt with specifically. The other sixteen were not mentioned, but the following clause was recommended to be included in the Constitution:

"At the end of the sixteenth clause, of the second section, seventh article, add, 'and to provide, as may become necessary, from time to time, for the well managing and securing the common property and general interests and welfare of the United States in such manner as shall not interfere with the governments of individual States,

64 LIBERTY vs. EQUALITY

in matters which respect only their internal police, or for which their individual authority may be competent.'"

This is the first appearance of the General Welfare Clause in Madison's *Journal*, and it was submitted to cover sixteen suggestions of Madison and Pinckney. Now if we follow the subsequent actions of the Convention, we find that ten of the sixteen suggested powers, such as patents, letters of mark and reprisal, copyrights, were later voted upon and were included specifically in the Constitution.

Thus, on September 17, 1787, when the proposed Constitution was agreed upon all the propositions which were before the Committee of Detail at the time when it advanced the General Welfare Clause were specifically settled with the exception of

1. to grant charters of incorporation in cases where the public good may require them and the authority of a single state be incompetent.
2. to regulate stages on the post roads.
3. to establish a university.
4. to encourage by premiums and provisions the advancement of useful knowledge.
5. to establish seminaries for the promotion of literature and the arts and sciences.
6. to establish public institutions, rewards and immunities for the promotion of agriculture, commerce, trades, and manufactures.

From the discussion of the power of incorporation[3] it was evident that this referred to roads, canals, banks, etc. Thus, those remaining proposals had to do with internal improvements, public works, and education. The Convention could have omitted the General Welfare Clause, but it did not. In fact it was moved from the end of the section to the beginning. This must be significant. Either the Convention in trying to settle certain miscellaneous problems hit upon this clause, and thought it an idea worth perpetuating; or else rather than force the issue of federal support of public works and education, deliberately left the gate open.

Four years later, Alexander Hamilton in his Report on Manufactures (to Congress, December 5, 1791) discussed this clause as follows:

"The terms 'general welfare' were doubtless intended to signify more than was expressed or imported in those which preceded; otherwise numerous exigencies incident to the affairs of a nation would have been left without a provision. The phrase is as comprehensive as any that could have been used, because it was not fit that the constitutional authority of the Union to appropiate its revenues should have been restricted within narrower limits than the 'general welfare', and because this necessarily embraces a vast

[3] Hunt: *The Writings of James Madison*, N. Y., 1903, IV, pp. 452–53.

variety of particulars, which are susceptible neither of specification nor of definition.

"It is, therefore, of necessity, left to the discretion of the National Legislature to pronounce upon the objects which concern the 'general welfare' and for which, under that description, an appropriation of money is requisite and proper. And there seems to be no room for a doubt that whatever concerns the general interests of learning, of agriculture, of manufactures, and of commerce, are within the sphere of the national councils, as far as regards an application of money." [4]

In 1799, in his Report to the House of Delegates of the State of Virginia on the justification of the Virginia Resolutions on the Alien and Sedition Acts, Madison takes direct issue with Hamilton on the above interpretation. At that time, twelve years after the Convention and more than forty years before the release of the *Journal,* Madison seems to refer to the General Welfare Clause as being merely a copy of a similiar clause in the old Articles of Confederation.

I wonder if Madison's memory in 1799 is more to be trusted than his *Journal* written at the time of the Convention. For in the *Journal* he repeats that on Sepember 14, 1787, he again moved that the power of incorporation be conferred on Congress, and the vote was lost because

[4] Lodge: *op. cit.,* III, 371–72.

as Mr. King said, it was unnecessary, and on the same day he and Pinckney again proposed the university, and the motion was lost, Gouverneur Morris saying "it is not necessary." This use of the words "not necessary" in Madison's *Journal* means that it is already implied in the Constitution.

Following the adoption of the Constitution, and the beginnings of the new government, great interest in general education was expressed by all the leaders. Washington proposed a national university, and Jefferson, Madison and Monroe all submitted recommendations to Congress for national subsidy of public schools. They urged an amendment to the Constitution to make this power perfectly plain.

Thus the Fathers of the Republic had a definite aim to bring liberty into life in the new nation. They projected a government which would never degenerate into tyranny. They guarded liberty of the person and security of property. They guaranteed freedom of speech and of the press, and religious liberty. They kept the government out of business. They firmly believed in the cultivation of education as the "great bulwark of republican government."

All the Fathers of the Constitution believed in liberty. Hardly any of them seemed to believe in equality. The great advocate of equality, Thomas Jefferson, was in France at the time, and even he expressed doubts about equality amongst artisans and factory workers in the great cities.

When the proposed constitution was sent to the Thirteen States for ratification, Madison, Hamilton and Jay wrote *The Federalist*, a series of papers advocating the proposed constitution. But no reference was made to the ideal of equality.

A number of the leaders were quite outspoken in their opposition to the idea. Consider the following statements of Hamilton:

"All communities divide themselves into the few and the many. The first are the rich and the well-born, the other the mass of the people. The voice of the people has been said to be the voice of God; and however generally this maxim has been quoted and believed, it is not true in fact. The people are turbulent and changing; they seldom judge or determine right. Give, therefore, to the first class a distinct, permanent share in the government. . . . Nothing but a permanent body can check the imprudence of democracy."[5]

"It is worthy of particular remark, that, in general, women and children are rendered more useful, and the latter more early useful, by manufacturing establishments, than they would otherwise be. Of the number of persons employed in the cotton manufactories of Great Britain it is computed that four sevenths, nearly, are women

[5] Lodge: *op. cit.*, I, p. 382.

FREE AND EQUAL

and children, of whom the greatest proportion are children, and many of them of a tender age." [6]

"Your people, sir, your people is a great beast." [7]

Consider also some of the statements of John Adams:

"Take away thrones and crowns from among men and there will soon be an end to all dominion and justice. There must be some adventitious properties infused into the government to give it energy and spirit, or the selfish, turbulent passions of men can never be controlled. This has occasioned that artificial splendor and dignity that are to be found in the courts of many nations. The people of the United States may probably be induced to regard and obey the laws without requiring the experiment of courts and titled monarchs." [8]

"If these words are true, no well-ordered commonwealth ever existed; for we read of none without a nobility; no, not even one that I can recollect without a hereditary nobility. . . . It would be an improvement in the affairs of society, if hereditary legal descent could be avoided; and this experiment the Americans have tried. But in this case a nobility must and will exist, though

---

[6] Lodge: *op. cit.*, III, p. 314.
[7] *Cf.* Merriam, *American Political Theories*, 123–127; H. Adams, *United States*, I, 83–89.
[8] Quoted in Parrington, *The Colonial Mind*, Harcourt, Brace, N. Y., 1927, p. 311.

without the name, as really as in countries where it is hereditary."[9]

It is true that the Constitution prohibited titles of nobility. It is true that the Bill of Rights gave equality before the law, but in the main, there was general sympathy, among the leaders at least, with the ideas of Hamilton and Adams. There were not many very rich people. The poor and destitute emigrated to the West. Class lines were not too sharply drawn. Yet in 1800 not one adult male in five had the right to vote; and qualifications of property and wealth were prerequisites for office holding in many of the states. As late as 1890 one had to be worth $5,000 to be eligible to become a candidate for the governorship of Massachusetts.

But the new United States could not long ignore the problem of equality. It was being intensified by the Industrial Revolution which the country was beginning to experience.

Prior to this time the bulk of manufacturing (as the name implies) had been done by hand. When spinning and weaving were performed on the wheel and the treadle loom, the work could be done as well at home as anywhere else. In fact it was more advantageous to work at home for the weaver could run a small farm in summer, weave on rainy days and in the winter, and sell or trade

[9] Adams, Charles Francis: *The Works of John Adams,* Boston, 1851, VI, p. 124.

the cloth himself. When Samuel Slater, who had worked in factories in England, reproduced from memory the carefully guarded secrets of the power machines, he started the factory system in America. The isolated worker could not compete with steam or water, and many machines could be driven as conveniently as one, provided they were under one roof. This meant that the worker lost his independence. No longer did he own his own loom. No longer was he his own boss. Along with many others he became a factory hand, and worked for the owner who bought the raw material, paid a wage, and sold the product. The Industrial Revolution put many men into the power of one; it brought country people to the city; it crowded unsanitary tenements; it stimulated vice and immorality and increased disease; and it forced miserable conditions of work and long hours of labor upon men, women and children.

James Truslow Adams writes of these times as follows:

"The New Englanders, however, now busy starting their new textile mills solved the problem for the generation of 1800 onward. For various reasons there was much distress among the small farmers, which accounted for the great emigration to the West. Many, however, could not emigrate, because of abject poverty or other causes. To operate their new machines, the mill owners exploited these conditions by seizing on the wives and children of impoverished farmers. 'In collecting our help,' wrote one, 'we are obliged to employ poor families, and generally those having the greater number of children.' Tending machines, wrote another, did not require men, but was better done by girls of from six to twelve years of age.... In one Rhode Island plant in 1801, Josiah Quincy found one hundred of them at work, for from twelve to twenty-five cents a day, there being a 'dull dejection in the countenances of all of them.' Possibly three quarters of the operatives were young women, but sometimes an entire family let themselves out. In one case, for example, a man signed a contract for $5.00 a week for himself, $2.00 for his sixteen-year-old son, $1.50 for his thirteen-year-old son, $1.25 for his daughter of twelve, $.83 for his boy of ten, $2.33 for his sister, $1.50 for her son of thirteen, and $.75 for her daughter of eight." [10]

On June 15, 1825, the Senate of the State of Massachusetts received a report of a survey of hours of children's labor and their opportunity for schooling. Instances were cited of 354 boys and 584 girls. Six worked only eleven hours a day, many at least twelve hours, and most from daylight to dark. Only 27 boys and 71 girls had any opportunity whatsoever for schooling, and even this was reported as "for four weeks" or "for eight

[10] Adams, James Truslow: *op. cit.*, p. 131.

weeks" or "for two months for lack of water" which kept the machines from turning. Scattered through the records of legislatures, patriotic societies and like organizations of the time can be found analyses of conditions, and protests and evidences of pressure exerted upon lawmakers for the correction of evils. The Committee on Education of the New England Association of Farmers, Mechanics, and other Working Men concluded their report of April 3, 1832, as follows:

"Your committee cannot therefore without the violation of a solemn trust, withhold their unanimous opinion, that the opportunities allowed to children and youth employed in manufactories, to obtain an education suitable to . . . American freemen, and the wives and mothers of such, are altogether inadequate to the purpose; that the evils complained of are unjust and cruel; and are no less than the sacrifice of the dearest interests of thousands of the rising generation of our country, to the cupidity and avarice of their employers. And they can see no other result in prospect, as likely to eventuate from such practices than generation on generation, reared up in profound ignorance, and the final prostration of their liberties at the shrine of a powerful aristocracy. . . .

"RESOLVED: that a committee of vigilance be appointed in each state represented in this convention, whose duty it shall be . . . to get up memorials to the Legislatures of their respective states praying . . . for some wholesome regulations with regard to the education of children and youth employed in manufactories."[11]

It is at this point that we begin to see the important rôle that education plays in the battle for liberty and equality. Here are the leaders of early America imbued with the idea of liberty. They build the best government that they know. They guarantee liberty in law. Yet they all agree that something else is needed,—a system of education for all, supported at public expense. Most of these same leaders were not enamoured of the idea of equality, beyond a mere equality before the law and an equal voice in government; and undoubtedly the theoretical equalitarians lost some of their enthusiasm in watching the horrors of the French Revolution where liberty was sacrificed on the altar of equality.

Nevertheless there were lovers of equality in America,—the common people. The Industrial Revolution had sapped the independence of the worker and had inflamed the cupidity of an exploiting class. There was too great injustice. There was beginning that creation of a class of opulence and a class of destitutes which Rousseau feared. No matter what the liberals said philo-

[11] Commons, J. R. *A Documentary History of American Industrial Society*, Cleveland, 1910, V, pp. 198–99.

sophically, the common people were going to do something about it.

Just as all Americans fought for liberty, the common people fought for equality. The regulation of conditions of labor and the development of a system of free public schools were not humanitarian ideas conceived by men like Horace Mann and Henry Barnard to be conferred by benevolent tax-payers upon a grateful public. Far from it. These reforms were the result of an organized demand by the people themselves. The people were angry. They knew what they wanted —and they got it.

What the equalitarians wanted was regulation of conditions of labor,—and a free public school system open to all the children of all the people and supported at public expense. This would give *equality of opportunity,* which is the equality that people wanted in that day. Exactly the same thing was stated by the liberals, as their ideal of the surest perpetuation of liberty. For once both liberty and equality met on the common ground of education.

Yet the battle for the free public school was not easily won. Americans have always had to fight other Americans both for liberty and equality.

Despite all these conflicts, however, the young United States worked out its problems pretty well. After a nervous start, and much confusion, the Federal government took hold and gained sufficient power. The courts began to give justice, just as had been planned. The suffrage was gradually extended. The public school system took its form, expanded as the country expanded, and increasingly approached offering real equality of opportunity. The unemployed, created by periodic panics, were absorbed by the spacious frontier. The slavery controversy and the Civil War were survived. Great industrial genius, countless inventions and enormous natural resources combined to create great wealth; and despite the fact that there were labor troubles, Coxey's armies and the like, a sort of liberty and equality was enjoyed by all. Certainly we enjoyed more than any other country in the world.

We were suddenly awakened from this dream of bliss by the unexpected arrival of the Power Age.

IV

LIBERTY, EQUALITY AND THE POWER AGE

"Voices of discouragement join with the voices of other social faiths to assert that an irreconcilable conflict has arisen in which Liberty must be sacrificed upon the altar of the Machine Age."

HERBERT HOOVER.

IV

LIBERTY, EQUALITY AND THE POWER AGE

FIFTEEN years ago in Nanking in China I used to be disturbed until far into the night by the clatter of treadle looms. At home the father of the family was at his work weaving the thread into brocades, and the wife and children, young and old assisted him. Just as in the days of Silas Marner, the worker worked for himself, purchased the thread, sold the cloth and lived an independent, though meager, existence. Life was similar to that in the American colonies before Samuel Slater's feat of memory inaugurated the Industrial Revolution.

But even in China of that time this change was imminent. While Nanking's weavers worked at their hand looms, Shanghai already stood wreathed in factory smoke; and miserable conditions of work, long hours, labor by women and children and ill health had overtaken the workers, country people unaccustomed to this new city life. It was plain that the educational system of China would soon have to adjust itself to this fundamental change in the life of the people; and

I felt considerable satisfaction that this hard process had already taken place in the United States a century before, that the problem had long since emerged, that the transition had been safely made and the educational implications fully realized.

It was something of a shock, therefore, after reading *Middletown* by the Lynds and *Recent Economic Changes* by the Hoover Commission,—to learn that my complacency had no foundation in fact. "The present situation of the United States," writes Professor Gay of Harvard, ". . . may be regarded in future times as but one interesting stage in a lengthening series of somewhat similar episodes characterizing the economic history of this and other modern nations. The Industrial Revolution, of which this stage is a part, was not merely a sudden burst of industrial and commercial activity, occurring in England just before the threshold of the nineteenth century and spreading by transmission or diffusion at successive intervals to other countries. It was rather a new organic growth, utilizing new powers over nature and expanding over the world with an uneven but continuing acceleration. . . . The successive phases of its development we have only begun to analyze."[1] Thus the Industrial Revolution is not a thing of the past. The period from 1780 to 1830 was only the start. The changes from "that primi-

[1] *Recent Economic Changes*, N. Y., 1929, I, p. 8.

LIBERTY, EQUALITY AND POWER AGE 81

tive, equalitarian, individualistic democracy produced by the log cabin, free land and isolation" begun late in the Eighteenth Century, have continuously progressed since that time, and in the period since the War have modified our society with increasing and heightened results. The full effects have not yet been reached. Important changes are still in the making. We are passing one of the great milestones of history. A society is developing different from anything that man has ever seen. We are entering upon a new world.

Apparently the changes will be greater and the strains more tense than in the last great period of change that we experienced. At that time a society which was getting along well found itself in trouble. A new government had been designed to give liberty to all and a certain measure of equality. The introduction of the factory system brought problems with it that were greater than the old order was able to solve. Liberty began to vanish from part of the people, and equality to become little more than a name. To keep liberty and to give equality, and to prevent them from killing each other off, the United States of 1820–40 had to take severe measures, to begin to control certain aspects of business, and to develop a nation-wide school system. The reforms came many years after the problems became apparent.

This new age, the Power Age as it is beginning

to be called, has come upon us unannounced; and just as in the Industrial Revolution a century ago, it is putting a tremendous strain upon the measures which our country has developed to give us liberty and equality. The old compromises do not seem to work. Part of our people state that equality is nothing but a myth. The rest say that liberty has vanished from the scene.

What the United States needs at the moment is a good look into the future. What is this Power Age? What will be its characteristics? What will be the conditions of life? Will liberty be possible? Will equality be possible? Can there be any compromise between the two?

It is to put this problem before us that I now enter the realm of conjecture. I know how dangerous it is to prophesy; and I know how foolish these words may look to the reader fifty years hence, if by chance they happen to be preserved until that time. What I propose to do, is in brief and sketchy form, to try to predict certain characteristics of the Power Age; and I shall do this, by analysing these characteristics as they appeared in the old Agrarian Age, as they were modified in the Industrial Revolution, and as they appear to have been changing during the last few years. If there is a steady trend, from past to present, I assume that this change can be projected into the future. By the Agrarian Age I mean the days of Silas Marner in England,

LIBERTY, EQUALITY AND POWER AGE

Massachusetts when Franklin was a boy, the Middle West when Lincoln split rails and the life described by Hamlin Garland in "Boy Life on the Prairie." By the Industrial Revolution I mean the England that Sir Robert Peel tried to reform, the Massachusetts of 1830, and the Shanghai of today. By the Power Age I mean what we are likely to become in a few years, if present trends continue unchecked.

In the interests of clarity and economy of time and space, these trends are presented in three tables—Table A, "PRODUCTION" appears on the following page; Table B, "GOVERNMENT" appears on page 88; and Table C, "LIFE OF THE PEOPLE" on page 93.

The central feature of the Power Age is the tremendous change in production caused by the development of technology. Just as the invention of the steam engine and the power machines for spinning and weaving changed the whole fabric of English society, so the development of modern technology is bringing even more fundamental alterations in all aspects of our social structure. There had to be certain developments and discoveries before modern technology could get under way. First, it was necessary to find out how to transmit power over long distances and how to create great central generating stations capable of furnishing this power at low cost. Second, machines "of great force and intricate

A. PRODUCTION

	THE AGRARIAN AGE What once was!	THE INDUSTRIAL REVOLUTION What we passed through!	THE POWER AGE What apparently is coming!
TYPE	Manufacture by individuals in small groups at home.	The factory system.	Tremendous organizations for production combining under one control, raw materials, fuel, transport, communication, fabrication and distribution.
PLACE	In every village.	Centered at sources of power.	Highly centralized in great establishments, after mergers of rival organizations and abandonment of local factories.
RATE	Slow production. Much use of man power per unit produced.	More rapid production. Less man power per unit produced.	High speed production. Very little man power per unit produced. Beginnings of automatic production.
EMPLOYMENT	A job for anyone who wants to work. Emigration for excess workers. Free land.	Rise of technological unemployment. Differentiation of processes. Frontier still open.	All of the workers idle some of the time. Some of the workers idle all of the time. Because of: Increasing technological unemployment. Mergers. Emphasis on younger workers. Over production. Closed frontier.
TEMPO	Long hours. Leisurely tempo. Rhythm of the seasons.	Increasing tempo. Long hours. Regimentation of life.	High speed. Short hours. Periodic shut downs.
CONTROL	Individual free, but often under governmental regulation as to quality, price, apprenticeship.	Laissez-faire. Boss and worker. Exploitation. Strikes, boycotts, lockouts, etc.	Co-operative administration. Scientific management. Government control. Government ownership.

LIBERTY, EQUALITY AND POWER AGE

cleverness" had to be invented and constructed. Third, before these machines could be constructed the invention and construction of "vast and precise machine tools" was necessary. Fourth, men had to learn to construct "precise measuring instruments" without which production in great quantity by machines would of necessity be confined to products of a cruder sort. In the last few years, all four of these essentials have been provided,—power, machines, machine tools and a great variety of precise measuring instruments; and thus modern business enterprise is able to bring "under one central control all necessary raw materials and fuel resources, the mechanism of transport and communication, the mechanism of fabrication and assembling of parts to produce the completed article of consumption."[2] Engineers and technologists have established techniques whereby many of the necessities of man can be produced by "straight line" production methods, in vast quantities, at low cost, and with little human labor. They state that these methods of production can be far more widely applied, so that in time almost everything that we consume or enjoy can be produced in this way.

The little workrooms in the home and the small manufactory in the village gave way to the factory situated near a waterfall, or built near a seaport

[2] This analysis is based upon *The Great Technology* by Harold Rugg.

or river where fuel could easily be brought. In the future many of these centers will disappear, and the tendency in turn will be to concentrate much of the production in great manufacturing enterprises in great cities.

Production used to be slow. Men labored long over weaving one piece of cloth, over blowing one bottle, over making one plate. The factory system increased the rate of production; and in the last few years this rate has increased enormously. We appear to be coming to a time when much less human labor will be required; and in some lines, production has become almost automatic.

This means that employment will become much less regular. Once upon a time most people could get a job, or in the event of failure to do so, could emigrate or move to free land in the West. To a decreasing degree this was true during the Industrial Revolution. Certainly if present conditions continue unchecked, *all* of the workers will be idle some of the time and some of the workers idle *all* of the time. According to the Technocrats, everything that our people could use or abuse could be produced by straight-line methods by the adults of the population between 21 and 45 years of age working a few hours a day, for a few days a week. Probably we should not take so extreme a statement seriously; but the trends appear to lead in that direction.

LIBERTY, EQUALITY AND POWER AGE

The leisurely work from daylight to dark of the Agrarian Age, tempered by reduced activity in the winter, gave way to the regimentation of life under the factory system. In the Power Age, it looks as though many of us would work furiously at high speed performing repeatedly some intricate operation to supplement the work of a whirring machine for brief periods; and then sit idle for much of the time.

There is also a change on the horizon in the control and management of production. In the Agrarian Age, the individual producer was his own boss; although under most European governmental systems he was subject to government regulations as to the quality of his product, the price at which he could sell, the apprentices that he could admit to the organization, the conditions under which he could transport goods and the like. The Industrial Revolution was the period of laissez-faire, when government stepped out and let things take their course under competition. It appears that laissez-faire will be under very important criticism in the Power Age. This leads us to Table B, "GOVERNMENT," found on the following page.

These conditions of production, which we have forecast for the Power Age, are not very startling. Most of them are found in the United States today during the depression;—and their effect has been to cause great distrust of the doctrine

B. GOVERNMENT

	THE AGRARIAN AGE What once was!	THE INDUSTRIAL REVOLUTION What we passed through!	THE POWER AGE What apparently is coming!
PHILOSOPHY	Government rules and regulates sale of agricultural products, quality of manufactures, grants, rights of monopoly, regulates transportation, sale and price.	Development of laissez-faire. Free competition, free production.	Growing distrust of laissez-faire. Increasing government regulation, codes, pressure. Distinct movement toward government ownership and operation.
FORM	Government of the many by the few.	Growth of parliaments, and democratic government.	Tendency toward dictatorship.

of laissez-faire and consequently to center far greater power in government. This has been the tendency of both radicals and conservatives.

The conservatives think of these conditions as being merely a repetition of the past. There have been many previous depressions. One followed the French and Indian War; one followed the War of 1812, and others came in 1837, 1857, 1873 and 1892. Each was severe. Farmers received little for their products. Land was sold for taxes. Banks failed. Savings were swept away. Starving people roamed the streets. Everywhere there was discouragement and dread of the future. On many previous occasions in America, it was freely predicted that we were at the end of an era, that civilization had crashed, and that the dark ages

LIBERTY, EQUALITY AND POWER AGE 89

lay ahead. Each time, say the conservatives, we recovered, to surge on to greater heights.

The conservative thinks that we are merely repeating the experience of the past. As has happened repeatedly, social memory is short. There was too much faith in the future, too much optimism. More was borrowed than could be repaid and more produced than could be consumed. In the days of prosperity men overreached themselves, and in days of depression they must wait to catch up. If we only wait for a time, goods will wear out, and food stocks will be consumed; then with the supply diminished and the demand increasing, prices will rise, factories will be opened, employees will go back to work, farmers will receive better prices for wheat and cotton, and all will be well.

The trouble is that the starving cannot wait, so even the conservative lends his support to measures of palliation. He contributes liberally toward the relief of misery, he advocates unemployment insurance, he favors "made work" whether privately or by the government. He would like to prevent the recurrence of a depression, so he supports government planning, and other government efforts towards co-ordination of industry, agriculture and transportation, provided it is on a "voluntary" basis. He even advocates government ownership and control of certain industries. He supports such measures as the regulation of banks, money, credit and sale of securities; but he tries to hold the government within bounds. Hopeful for recovery, even in times of deep depression, he concentrates his efforts on palliation of the present, and the improvement of the economic system at least to the extent of softening the blow of recurring panics. He agrees that depressions are probably inevitable even when laissez-faire is restricted; for the conservative I have described is moving from laissez-faire to government control.

But there are those who believe that the conditions of the Power Age constitute a permanent change; they have pondered the consequences of these changes; and they have some very startling suggestions to make. They say that this depression which we are passing through is not like any depression that has gone before. Rugg states that it "is not a mere fourteenth installment-paying time, (referring to 13 previous depressions); it is a day of inventory and final reckoning." Millions of people are out of work, and permanently so, for a variety of reasons. Machines have taken their place. Small factories have been closed and moved away. Unrestricted competition has caused more to be produced than people could consume, even if they could purchase. But they have no money. When they are out of work their income ceases, and more factories shut down. It is a vicious circle that public works, unemployment relief, loans to business, and processing taxes can palliate only for a while. Competition must be controlled. Greed must be crushed. Someone must take hold of the government and run it with an iron hand. Set the economist and sociologist to work to find out what the people need and want. Give the engineers and technologists the problem of producing just this amount and no more. See that the products are distributed to the consumers. Divide up the work evenly among all. Abolish our present system of prices, money, charity, insurance and savings. This is the Utopia that New America, the Technocrats and many others hold before us. However accurate or inaccurate the data behind their judgments, however optimistic their predictions, however naïve their proposals, their point of view must be reckoned with. For it has as its aim equality, and once again, just as with Robespierre, they are willing to slaughter liberty to get it.

One is reminded of the Comte de Ségur, quoted by Walter Alison Phillips in his introduction to Gaxotte's *The French Revolution* (who by the way made up this quotation by taking several phrases from different places in the first chapter).

"We laughed mockingly at the old fashions . . . All that was old seemed to us tiresome and ridiculous . . . Voltaire carried away our intellects; Rousseau touched our hearts; it gave us a secret pleasure to see them attack an old structure which seemed to us gothic and ridiculous, and so, without regret for the past, without fear for the future, we walked gaily on a carpet of flowers that hid the abyss beneath our feet."

So in the Power Age, conservative and radical unite to increase the part that government will play in our lives. We are moving rapidly away from Jefferson's idea of a "frugal" government. The driving force is the conviction that in the quest for liberty we have sacrificed equality. What compromise can the future make?

Table C, "LIFE OF THE PEOPLE," which appears on the following page, speaks for itself. It depicts a continuing growth away from independence to interdependence, from self sufficiency to dependence upon others, from individual to community life. It shows that men and women are going to have a new kind of life, fast and furious work in industry at highly complicated tasks, coupled with long periods of inaction. Some think the nervous strain will be too great for the human constitution; yet my impression is that this is the kind of life lived by primitive tribes.

The real problem is, of course, the problem that societies have struggled with over and over again in the course of history, and they have without exception failed. It is the question of solving the problem of a civilization based upon slavery. The citizens of Athens let the slaves do the work, and they went to pieces. The citizens of the

C. LIFE OF THE PEOPLE

	THE AGRARIAN AGE What once was!	THE INDUSTRIAL REVOLUTION What we passed through!	THE POWER AGE What apparently is coming!
STANDARD OF LIVING	A "pain economy" Not enough to go around. Simple standard of living.	Low standard of living among workers. Much higher standard among the wealthy. Rise of an affluent middle class.	A "pleasure economy." Plenty. Rise of salesmanship, advertising, partial payments. Universal ownership of automobiles. radios. washing machines. Less universal ownership of bath tubs and books.
INTERDEPENDENCE	Family or small community self sufficient. Little recourse to trade. Barter. Personal relationships.	Increasing trade — but relatively few commodities.	Complete interdependence. ready-made clothes. baker's bread. canned food. community laundry. community kitchen. Great variety of commodities. Money — not barter. Impersonal relations.
LEISURE	Work for all the family all the time, except for a few holidays. Simple pleasures and few.	At first work for men, women and children, changing to work for adults; then shorter hours. Beginnings of commercialized amusement.	Work mostly by men and women from 21 to 45. Short hours. Few days a week. Long periods of idleness. Increasing nervous disease. Increase of problem of care of youth and those 45 and older.

Power Age will let the machines do the work. Will they decline and fall?

This curious type of life which our children are likely to live constitutes our greatest danger. If we but use our intelligence, it may constitute our greatest blessing,—the solution to the other problems which the Power Age has raised.

In conclusion, the Power Age has put two great problems to us. In the search for liberty and equality, and in the effort to compromise between the two, America once adopted two policies, one of a frugal, democratic government, the other of laissez-faire. The effect was to emphasize liberty rather than equality. A change must be made. To secure greater equality, power is becoming increasingly centered in the government; and laissez-faire is giving way to a planned and controlled economy. The time is not far distant when the pendulum will have swung too far, and equality will be emphasized to the exclusion of liberty, as is the case in Russia today. During the last great period of social change, the compromise between the two ideals was effected through our system of education. Can this again be the case in the Power Age?

V

LIBERTY AND LEARNING

"What spectacle can be more edifying or more seasonable, than that of Liberty and Learning, each leaning on the other for their mutual and surest support?"

JAMES MADISON.

V

LIBERTY AND LEARNING

"The Revolution" is a proper noun in American history. It refers directly to the War of Independence. When we say "before the Revolution" we are referring to Colonial times when our fathers were subject to the Crown. "After the Revolution" indicates all the years following the conclusion of peace in 1783. But it is possible that this term may come to have a different meaning. It may be that future school children will connect the word "revolution" with the events beginning in the year 1933, which introduced the New Deal and the fundamental changes in the government of the United States consequent upon it. That year may mark a turning point in the history of the United States, the end of one era and the beginning of another. Possibly 1933 will come to be known as a pivotal date, like 1776 or 1789; not to commemorate the formal proclamation of independence from royalty or the beginning of revolt against tyranny, but rather to mark the time, when, to meet the problems of the Power Age, Americans peacefully and without violence bartered a part of their liberty to secure greater equality.

For the democratic landslide of 1932 which brought President Roosevelt into office was the result of a campaign waged for the ideal of equality. The farmers had been badly treated, labor had not received its just desserts, the "forgotten man" was to be remembered. Certainly the depression had carried us into the depths. It was apparent that the old order had failed.

For we can agree with Tugwell that "March 4 last may be taken . . . as the low point in our history. Borne down by one disaster after another, overcome by an almost complete paralysis of will, we stood bowed, a nation without a leader, lost. Business crept to a standstill. Millions of blameless people shuffled in breadlines. Every bank in the land was closed. Groups of farmers in open revolt defied their creditors and the law. We hardly knew whether we had a government any longer. None of us who lived through the tension and hysteria of that gray inauguration day will ever forget it."[1] Blind, unreasoning fear held the country in its grip. There was a hush upon the sidewalks of New York. It was for a Paris like this that Ste. Genevieve prayed; it was for such a Rome that Horatius held the bridge. But it was no Attila, no Tarquin that we had to fear.

[1] Tugwell, R. G., "The Ideas Behind the New Deal," *New York Times,* July 16, 1933.

LIBERTY AND LEARNING

The enemy was within our gates, within our hearts. Competition unrestricted, selfishness uncontrolled, stupidity and turpitude had almost brought the nation to its knees. And it was this enemy that the new government mobilized its forces to defeat. Whatever criticism may be made of the Roosevelt administration, whatever objection may be raised to the developments at Washington, we must always remember the state of affairs that March and be grateful for the courage and resolution that were shown. For we thought we were lost and we were saved. Hope had vanished and confidence was restored. In the short space of one hundred days all was changed. We must always be thankful for that.

It was a novel task that confronted the government, one far more complicated than waging war. There was little precedent upon which to act. Tugwell put the problem as follows:

"The government's house had to be set in order and its credit reëstablished. The faith of the people in their banks had to be restored. Food and shelter had to be provided for great masses of the hungry and homeless, and this task was but a detail in view of the longer task beyond. The longer task was to get the wheels of industry turning, to put millions back to work, to restore to the people of this country a reasonable assurance of security.

That is still the test by which all our present efforts must in the end be judged. Unless we can make people feel again that for the man who wants to work, work will be provided; unless we can, by a balanced allocation of enterprise, assure a decent standard of living for all who do their part; unless—not with words but with jobs—we can make the ordinary man and woman feel that their lives and efforts are wanted in this society, then our plans will have failed." [2]

Of course such a program was beyond the experience of a government planned to operate under an economy of laissez-faire. It was one thing to direct the army, the navy, and the foreign service, to operate the post office and the national parks, to maintain lighthouses, and to deepen rivers and harbors. It was quite another thing to restore buying power to the farm, to raise price levels, to establish means of self-control for agriculture and industry, to control competition, to enlarge incomes, and to secure the people against risk. The old machinery could not do this. The New Deal required a new dealer. In order to deal, it was necessary for one person to have the entire deck in his hands. This is the essence of government under the New Deal. There is a double concentration. The Federal Government assumed powers far beyond anything hitherto contemplated, and within the Federal Government itself these powers are centered in the Executive.

Thus the New Deal first sought to remove

[2] *Ibid.*

from private individuals, from localities, and from states, and to concentrate at Washington, the power of national planning, the control of exploitation and competition, and the management of the huge combinations that must prevail if the wealth which they develop is to be justly distributed.

The second step was to confer these powers upon the Executive. Under the Reorganization Act, the National Economy Act, the Relief Act, the Farm Act, the National Industrial Recovery Act, and other acts of the one hundred days, at least seventy-seven powers were transferred to the Executive, among them the power to control and administer all business and industry; to govern production, prices, profits, competition, wages, and the hours of labor; to reapportion private wealth and income throughout the nation; to debase money on behalf of the debtor class; to produce inflation in the interest of certain classes; and "the power specifically to reduce the gold value of the dollar one-half—or, that is to say, the power, simply by proclamation, to double the price of everything that is priced in dollars, and to halve the value of every obligation payable in dollars, such as debts, bonds and mortgages, insurance policies, bank deposits." [3]

---

[3] The substance of this paragraph follows the analysis of Garet Garrett in *The Saturday Evening Post,* August 12, 1933 ("The Hundred Days").

These acts of the New Deal constitute the sharpest break with the past in the history of the United States. Our fathers set up a government of *laws,* not a government of men. The New Deal set up a government of *men,* not a government of laws. Our fathers set up a government with powers divided, between the states and the nation, between the three branches of the Federal Government, between the Senate and the House of Representatives. The New Deal concentrated these powers in the Executive. Truly we are living through a Revolution. To defeat a common enemy we have established what amounts to a dictatorship. The interesting feature of the New Deal is that the people on the whole seem to like it. If the President can deal the cards, let him deal. "If any man can play the pipes, in God's name let him play."

In the old days the American people would not have welcomed a dictatorship. Those who were brought up on the words of Locke, Montesquieu, and Rousseau, those who read Jefferson, Adams, and Monroe, those who were bred on Thomas Paine, Noah Webster, *The Federalist* and the other writings of Hamilton and Madison had aroused within them a love of freedom. It was of a "Sweet Land of Liberty" that they sang, of a "home of the brave and the free." They said, "Give me Liberty or give me Death." They set up a government of checks and balances, and they reserved to themselves, to their families, to their localities, and to their states all the power possible. The Constitution of the United States almost missed ratification because of what was believed to be too great a transfer of power. The student of history knows the origin of this love of liberty. From an examination of the records of the past he learns to appreciate the unhappiness of life under a despot, and the injustice of existence under a tyrant. He also learns what sometimes we forget, that economic tyranny is as bad as political and that they go together. The American Dream was not only an urge toward a new civilization. It was a flight from despotism, political and economic.

It is obvious, however, that nowhere in political science can one discover an ideal amount of power to entrust to a government. There is no set standard upon which wise men unanimously agree. Madison wrote to Jefferson in 1788, when they were discussing the merits of the proposed Constitution.

> It is a melancholy reflection that liberty should be equally exposed to danger whether the Government have too much or too little power, and that the line which divides these extremes should be so inaccurately defined by experience.

The government of the United States, checked and balanced, divided in various ways, was once capable of meeting most of its needs; but it could not function in the Civil War or in the World War. Dictatorial powers were granted to Lincoln and Woodrow Wilson. When the emergency ceased, the government resumed its normal aspect.

In the present crisis dictatorial powers have again been granted, and far more comprehensive functions have been assumed by the Federal Government. When our government had too little power, our liberties were in danger. Now that it is capable of meeting the needs of the day, should one fear degeneration into despotism? Americans won their liberty at a price of the lives, property, and efforts of many who have gone before. These liberties have been cherished and handed down to us. We must not trifle with this heritage. "Every free people," says Rousseau, "should remember this maxim, that tho' nations may acquire liberty, yet if once this inestimable acquisition is lost, it is absolutely irrecoverable."[4] Is it possible, then, to proceed under a dictatorship and at the same time guard our liberties?

Writers on governments agree that dictatorship unchecked will degenerate into tyranny. Various controls over dictatorship have been advanced. The simplest is to limit the time of office. The Romans elected a dictator for six months only, at the expiration of which time the powers re-

[4] Rousseau, Jean Jacques, *Miscellaneous Works,* London, 1763, V, p. 58.

verted. Rousseau, discussing dictatorship in a chapter in his *Social Contract,* admitted its need on rare occasions, and suggested guarding it as follows:

> After all, in whatever manner this important commission (dictatorship) may be conferred, it is of consequence to limit its duration to a short term; which should on no occasion be prolonged. In these conjectures, when it is necessary to appoint a dictator, the state is presently saved or destroyed, which causes being over, the dictator becomes useless and tyrannical.[5]

A number of the Acts of Congress, under the New Deal, guard our liberties by limiting the time. But one wonders whether the war parallel holds good. The enemy appears, the dictator is appointed, and the war is waged. If lost, there is no power left; if won, the crisis is past. But the war which the New Deal is fighting is waged against no temporary foe. It has assumed a task which is likely to be perpetual. It seems improbable that a government which presumes to manage industry, agriculture, and commerce in times of chaos can quietly step out and allow the same events to occur again.

A second guard against the degeneration of dictatorship into tyranny is the right to selection and removal. The American people elected President Roosevelt; their representatives in Con-

[5] *Ibid.,* V, pp. 167–68.

gress conferred power upon him. What was given can be taken away, in part at will, in part at stated intervals. It is not uncommon to confer dictatorial powers in other enterprises in our society. In our universities, in our public school systems, in our hospitals, in our waterworks, in our city engineering departments, we commonly grant large powers to administrative officers. There we have a government of men rather than a government of law. Whenever we like, we can guard against despotism by the power of removal and the power to select a successor. But in the case of the New Deal, there is at least room for doubt whether the power of selection and removal will constitute an adequate safeguard. The large powers over business will accrue not only to the individual incumbent, but will attach to the office as well. Of necessity a large and powerful group of subordinates will take over a share of authority. We know the avidity with which bureaucrats lap up power and build themselves into permanent possession of a function, an office, or a prerogative.

Another limitation of dictatorship is the direct circumscription of the powers conferred by written law. This, in a measure, we now have; but laws live by their interpretation as well as by their specific statements; and large powers are delegated by these laws as they stand. If our economic life is so managed as to appeal to the majority of Americans, Congress will hesitate to tamper with governmental procedures which are working well.

The only other possible limitation of dictatorship is education. When people are basely ignorant, no government is possible other than tyranny. Madison expressed this clearly in his letter to W. T. Barry in 1822:

A popular Government, without popular information, or the means of acquiring it, is but a Prologue to a Farce or a Tragedy, or, perhaps both. Knowledge will forever govern ignorance; and a people who mean to be their own Governors must arm themselves with the power which knowledge gives.

It is said that one reason for the early success of "the American experiment" was that the people knew something about self-government. Already they had had a century and a half of experience. They had built roads and bridges, they they had drained the swamps, they had supported schools, they had waged war, and they had taxed themselves to support these enterprises. By personal experience they had prepared themselves. It is also true that the problems of government were interesting to the people of that day; and the idea of building a new society on a new plan for new purposes had captured their imagination. The huge circulation of the pamphlets of Thomas Paine and Noah Webster testifies to the people's interest in and knowledge of governmental problems. The way in which Freneau and Alexander Hamilton discussed at length and in detail the issues of the debt, the bank and the Jay Treaty, as well as the issuance and effect of *The Federalist,* indicates that a significant part of the public would read if offered the opportunity, would discuss if presented the issues, and would act in accord. The debating society, the country store, even the taverns were forums for political speculation. Members of Congress felt themselves responsible to that part of their constituents who both knew and were concerned. The problems of government were not beyond the experience of those at home. The course had already been charted. No dictatorship was needed. No tyranny would be tolerated.

It is only when a brand-new problem comes along that the directors of government may have to go beyond the people. In Morley's *Life of Gladstone* there appears the following passage:

In the beginning of 1870 one of Mr. Gladstone's colleagues wrote of him to another, "I fear that he is steering straight upon the rocks.". . . The occasion was the measure for dealing with the land of Ireland. . . . The difficulty arose from the huge and bottomless ignorance of those in whose hands the power lay. Mr. Gladstone in the course of these discussions said, and said truly, of the learned Sir Roundell Palmer, that he knew no more of land tenures in Ireland than he knew of land tenures in the moon. At the beginning much the same might have been observed of the cabinet, of the two houses of Parliament, and of the whole mass of British electors. *No doubt one effect of this great ignorance was to make Mr. Gladstone dictator.* Still ignorance left all the more power to prejudice and interests.[6]

And it is always a temptation to meet "prejudice and interests" by force, to give (to use the phrase attributed to General Johnson) "a sock on the jaw."

Judged by the standards of education, there are four kinds of government. There are the ignorant leading the ignorant. This is tyranny. There are the ignorant leading the wise. This is a prelude to revolution. There are the wise leading the ignorant. This is dictatorship, possibly a benevolent autocracy. There are the wise leading the wise, giving liberty, and equality. This is the ideal of democracy.

If we review the present situation of the United States in this light, we see that the fight for equality has caused the Federal Government to assume power over functions and prerogatives hitherto in private hands; it has forced into public office men who know; it has compelled experimentation in the public direction of economic processes, sometimes by persuasion and propagandizing, sometimes by psychological or physical coercion. The leaders are none too certain of

[6] Morley, John, *The Life of William Ewart Gladstone,* London, 1903, II, p. 281.

their solutions, but the people know far less. Thus, at the moment with us, the wise or semiwise are leading the ignorant; and if this condition continues, it is almost certain to degenerate into tyranny. The problem is obvious.

If Americans love their liberty, and at the same time wish to secure equality, if they wish to avoid servitude in the future and at the same time remember the forgotten man, it is imperative that the knowledge of the people begin as soon as possible to approximate the knowledge of the leaders; that the people come to know the problems which their leaders are attempting to solve, sufficiently well to enable them to distinguish success from failure, to permit them to coöperate with a will rather than to yield obedience which must be blind and sullen because it is forced.

"And say finally," wrote Jefferson to Madison in 1787, "whether peace is best preserved by giving energy to the government, or information to the people. The last is the most certain, and the most legitimate engine of the government. Educate and inform the whole mass of the people. . . . They are the only sure reliance for the preservation of liberty."

This is the reason why the education of the people must be broadened in proportion as the government extends its interests and operations. The three R's might have been adequate for the "frugal government" of Thomas Jefferson; but they will certainly fall far short in helping our people to decide between the Liberty League, the New Deal, "Social Justice," and "Social Credit." In the recent campaign in the Province of Alberta in Canada, the people were asked to vote upon such questions as: How can the purchasing power of the consumer be increased? What is a just price, a fair wage, and how can they be regulated? When money is borrowed, should it be repaid? Should the government protect the borrower, and not the lender? Should the government advance money to stimulate production? How can new export markets be secured? Shall we distribute a dividend of $25.00 every month to every citizen?

When these questions come before the people of the United States shall we succumb to the blandishments of the modern socio-economic politician? Shall we support the economic theorist who proposes a remedy which, though he does not know it, has been tried repeatedly before, and always before has failed? We shall, if we are not armed with a thorough knowledge of political economics.

Education which will preserve our liberty must have as its aim the production of citizens who understand the society in which we have lived, the evil effects of selfishness, the social suicide of cut-throat competition, and the stupidity of narrow nationalism in a world society. It must hold as its purpose the production of citizens who will have the background and the knowledge sufficient to judge clearly the efforts of their leaders toward economic reconstruction. Our people may know the geography of South America; they may be able to list the capitals and rivers of the various states; they may even be able to spell correctly the words *economics* or *justice;* but they must in addition know what these facts and words mean.

Recently the milk producers of Connecticut have been striving to obtain seven cents a quart for four per cent milk. This granted, it now appears that the consumers are protesting because they are forced to pay fourteen cents. Is this spread in price just? Many factors must be taken into account to give the answer; but at the moment those in power who are trying to settle these differences are handicapped because, despite the fact that almost everybody uses milk, cream, or butter, no one—neither producer, processor, nor consumer—knows enough about the milk industry, its problems, its difficulties, either to make a wise decision or to support a wise decision if made. Until they know, either producers will be starved, processors will go out of business, consumers will be robbed, or they all will resort to a dictator to settle a problem which the people should be able to settle for themselves, and to enforce a solution which should need no enforcement beyond popular approval.

Wheat, cotton and corn, mining and manufacturing, trade and transportation, each has its manifold problems; each has been brought under the influence of the New Deal; and each is a challenge to all the knowledge and the wisdom of our leaders. The people should know.

The first demand made by the new conditions, then, should be a new kind of education, an education broader than that heretofore offered, one directed to the just assessment of the good and evil found in a society operating under laissez-faire in a fiercely competitive world.

Much attention should be paid to the methods suggested in the past and present with respect to possible reforms of the social and economic order. There is little new in the world. "New Deals" have been made time and time again. The citizen of America should know this; but he should also know full well that this is the first time in history that we have had a Power Age with the economy of plenty consequent upon it.

Not only must our philosophers, economists, and sociologists guide the curriculum toward an understanding of the New Deal and an appreciation of the problems of the Power Age, but there is the larger aspect which is, of course, the real problem. There was once a time when Americans loved liberty and feared tyranny; and it was towards perpetuating this spirit that the means of education of that day were directed. Sometimes it was the function of the school; more often of the less formal agencies of popular education. For the American who had just escaped from political and economic despotism kept "the fierce spirit of liberty" alive in his breast and took pains to arouse it in the hearts of his children.

For we know that the torch of liberty needs loving care. Unattended and unworshiped, it flickers and burns low. It was societies, clubs, reading rooms, pamphleteers, carrying on one of the most effective programs of adult education that the world has ever seen, that laid the foundations for the French Revolution. It was citizens' clubs and private, often secret, schools that by education liberated Bulgaria from the Turk. It was the American school, the American press, the American pulpit that gave the battle cry of freedom. We must revive that spirit today.

For the American people, having learned to clear the fields, build the railroads, mine the coal, and erect the factories—masters of all that around them lies—have been unable to control themselves. Rugged individualism, possible in a wise people, masters of their fate, broke down in the fever following the World War. We sought liberty and we lost equality. Now we have passed the crisis. We have chosen capable leaders and we have granted them large powers. If we read history aright, this may be the beginning of despotism. Mirabeau was followed by Robespierre and Napoleon. Kerensky gave way to Lenin and Stalin. Too often wisdom and public spirit are followed by greed for power. A people can guard against this succession by limiting the time of dictatorial power, by exercising the power of selection and removal, and by written law. None of these will be fully effective in our case. The only hope is education, widespread, thorough, comprehensive, and liberal. "What spectacle can be more edifying or more seasonable," wrote Madison, "than that of Liberty and Learning, each leaning on the other for their mutual and surest support?" What task more patriotic?

VI

LAISSEZ-FAIRE AND EDUCATION

"It is easy to prove that fortunes naturally tend to equality, and that their extreme disproportion either could not exist, or would quickly cease . . . if an entire freedom of commerce and industry were brought forward to supersede the advantages which prohibitory laws and fiscal rights necessarily give to the rich over the poor."

CONDORCET.

VI

LAISSEZ–FAIRE AND EDUCATION

Laissez-faire was an effort to remember the forgotten man. "This admirable system" as Condorcet put it, "so simple in its principles, which considers unrestricted liberty as the surest encouragement to commerce and industry, which will free the people from the intolerable burden of unequal taxation . . . which considers the prosperity and respect for the rights of the individual citizen as the real wealth and happiness of the nation . . ."—this application to economic life of the ideal of liberty,—was advanced by those who thought they were helping the common people.

The old system had been unjust. In ancient times, and certainly with the development of industry and commerce in the Middle Ages, it had become customary for governments to rule business. A man who wished to develop an industry, or to buy and sell goods, had to have the permission, if not the coöperation of the ruling power. The early history of Europe is crowded with illustrations of government direction and operation of industry, of government regulation of wages,[1] of government price-fixing,[2] of government restriction of production,[3] of government stimulation of production and trade,[4] of limitation of entrance to occupations and apprenticeships,[5] and of minute regulation of manufactures;[6] and there have been long periods in many countries of the world when most of the people lived in a constant time of depression because their economic opportunity was restricted by some prince, baron, guild, or mistery. Government had "governed too much" and the result was misery for the common man. When economic affairs started to go badly, there was always a group of government officials who considered it their duty to step in, reorganize and direct the agriculture, industry and commerce of the nation.

A good illustration of this process took place in France when Louis XIV was king. Under Richelieu and Mazarin conditions had become progressively worse. The taxing system had broken down. Out of 84,000,000 livres (dollars) exacted from the people in 1661, less than 23,000,000 reached the treasury. The government was virtually bankrupt. "The galleys and pris-

---

[1] Ashley, W. J., *An Introduction to English Economic History and Theory*, Pt. I, p. 193, London, 1888; Pt. II, p. 106, 7th Ed., London, 1912.
[2] *Ibid.*, Pt. I, pp. 182, 187, 190, 191; Pt. II, p. 160.
[3] *Ibid.*, Pt. II, p. 234.
[4] *Ibid.*, Pt. II, p. 199.
[5] *Ibid.*, Pt. I, p. 90; Pt. II, p. 160.
[6] *Ibid.*, Pt. II, p. 228.

ons were crowded, not with criminals, but with defaulting taxpayers and collectors." The people were impoverished. Despair stalked the land. Trade and agriculture were dead or fast dying. "The time had surely come," Sargent says, "for a drastic reform."

Colbert was the man of the hour. Immediately upon his accession he proceeded with utmost vigor, and supported fully by the king he embarked upon an economic program, a "new deal," which set France upon her feet. The revenues began to reach the treasury. It is not necessary to recall in detail the manner in which he simplified, and unified the taxing system and made it more just. What interests us is the way in which he tried to build up the economic strength of the nation. In his Edict of 1664 he states his purpose:

With a view to that end we determined to undertake in our own person the care of the administration of our finances, on the ground that these were the foundation of all that we could do for their (the people's) relief. But as we were well aware that the relief we were granting them could certainly diminish their wretchedness and give them some opportunity of existence, but could not bring affluence to them so that they might taste the sweets of that existence; and as we were aware that commerce alone can produce that great result, we have labored from the very beginning to lay the first foundations with a view to its reëstablishment.[7]

[7] Sargent, A. J.: *The Economic Policy of Colbert*, London, 1899, p. 44.

The successive acts in the reëstablishment of commerce were as follows:

Colbert removed the various obstacles to trade within the nation, systematizing and unifying duties, and building and repairing roads, bridges, and causeways.

He tried to develop France as a national unit, discouraging all trade from abroad. He imported skilled workmen, he established new industries, he guaranteed advantages and privileges to foreign manufacturers who would come to France.

He established the Royal Council of Commerce to advise the King with regard to trade; by circulars he introduced propaganda to encourage the people to manufacture and the men of wealth to invest in factories; he encouraged manufacturers by granting exclusive rights, by royal patronage, by royal subsidy.

He arranged for the government to control industry, to determine standards of quality and size. He prepared minute regulations with regard to almost every manufacture. These he enforced by inspection, "exposure," and confiscation.

To provide greater circulation, he debased the coinage.

Colbert revived France. He brought wealth to the kingdom. He provided employment for the people. In his Memoirs of 1680 he says with pride, "All these establishments have provided a living for an infinite number of persons and have kept money within the kingdom."

The plan succeeded for a time, but it could not last. As Sargent comments:

LAISSEZ-FAIRE AND EDUCATION

"Idleness and indifference in the people no less than their magistrates, the solid conservatism of ignorance, of natures content with things as they are and always have been, incapable even of realizing the infinite possibilities of improvement, these were barriers too strong for the forces of persuasion and good counsel."[8]

In place of relying upon information and advice, the government was compelled to resort to force. A huge bureaucracy was set up. Rules, regulations, and precedents interpreted by minor functionaries were substituted for the decision and wisdom of the genius, with the result that foreign trade began to decline and the people to complain. Here is an early example of a "squawk"[9] from the populace, that in a century led to the French Revolution.

Colbert left a bad heritage. A century later the people were plainly miserable. One need only read Turgot's experiences as Financial Administrator of the Limousin or Mirabeau on economic tyranny to learn the plight of the poor under the Corvée and Gabelle, the enforced labor of the under-privileged and sales taxes upon the necessities of the needy, and to appreciate the hopelessness of life, when trade, industry and business were in the grip of closed corporations operating under favor of the government, when prices, quality and standards were fixed by the central authority.

[8] *Ibid.*, p. 56.
[9] A word from General Johnson.

It was to help these poor people that the French economists advanced the idea of economic liberty. It was in the interests of social justice that Adam Smith promulgated the idea of laissez-faire. The simplicity and naturalness of the doctrine might make one think that it is the only system of government relative to industry that there has ever been;—but we must make no mistake. At the time it was a great discovery. The following statement from Adam Smith was the climax of his whole argument, and its acceptance by society was considered a great victory.

"All systems either of preference or of restraint, therefore, being thus completely taken away, the obvious and simple system of natural liberty establishes itself of its own accord. Every man, as long as he does not violate the laws of justice, is left perfectly free to pursue his own interest his own way, and to bring both his industry and capital into competition with those of any other man, or order of men. The sovereign is completely discharged from a duty, in the attempting to perform which he must always be exposed to innumerable delusions, and for the proper performance of which no human wisdom or knowledge could ever be sufficient; the duty of superintending the industry of private people, and of directing it towards the employments most suitable to the interest of the society. According to the system of natural liberty, the sovereign has only three duties to attend to; three duties of great importance, indeed, but plain and intelligible to common understandings: first, the

LAISSEZ–FAIRE AND EDUCATION 125

duty of protecting society from the violence and invasion of other independent societies; secondly, . . . the duty of establishing an exact administration of justice; and thirdly, the duty of erecting and maintaining certain public works and certain public institutions, which it can never be for the interest of any individual, or small number of individuals, to erect and maintain." [10]

I wonder what Quesnay, or Dupont de Nemours, or the elder Mirabeau, the "ami des hommes," or Turgot or Adam Smith, or Benjamin Franklin would think if they were to return to earth today. I fear that they would be greatly discouraged; for they would hear our economists talk of scrapping laissez-faire, when it is so new that it has hardly been tried; and they would listen to advocates of government control of industry and national planning speak as though they were the only advocates of equality, the only proponents of social justice, the only friends of the poor and the unfortunate. For our ancestors had seen government control of business, —temperate in the hands of a great man, become despotic in the power of the functionary; and they had never found human beings wise and disinterested enough to superintend "the industry of private people."

When progress toward social justice was blocked, when the common man had no chance,

[10] Smith, Adam, *The Wealth of Nations,* London, 1791, III, p. 42.

our fathers took the government *out* of business. Now that the path to social justice again appears to be blocked, and the common man has no chance, we are putting the government back *in!*

There is no doubt that something is wrong today. Even before 1929 we were far from social justice. The battle for liberty and equality had not been won. In the midst of plenty, there was starvation. Despite a nation-wide public school system, there was child labor. There were sweat shops and miserable conditions of work. Our fathers started out with a beautiful dream. They were going to build a nation to the pattern of liberty and equality; and the America of *Middletown* and of *Recent Economic Changes* and *Recent Social Trends* is the result. We mastered our environment; what we could not control was ourselves. Acquisitiveness and selfishness, primarily responsible for our failure, almost accomplished our undoing.

Now that we look back, it is plainly to be seen why we have departed so far from the medieval ideal of a fair price and a just wage,[11] why self-seeking and self-interest have become intensified in modern times. They are a by-product of the development of liberty and equality.

When we lived in an economy of scarcity, there

---

[11] Ashley, W. J., *op. cit.*, Pt. I, p. 139. Troeltsch, Ernst, *The Social Teaching of the Christian Churches,* Vol. I, pp. 319–20. New York, 1931.

was an insufficiency of the world's goods, there was not enough to go around, and he who did not get his foot in the trough probably perished. One would think that an economy of plenty would have diminished this trend. But the ideals of liberty and equality only accentuated it. When government monopolized industry and commerce there was no premium placed upon competition. When family status determined position in the world, the good citizen had merely acceptably to fill his appointed place. But the ideal of equality gives opportunity for personal advancement. Every daughter is a Cinderella, every son a possible Lincoln or Franklin. Life is a race. The ideal is "onward and upward." We are in the midst of a struggle. We must push. We must compete. We must exert every effort. We must surpass. And the foundation of economic liberty is competition. Neither liberty in business nor equality of opportunity would have been possible without the tremendous efforts put forth by men and women actuated by motives of self-interest. But what was once a virtue has become a vice; generosity has become buried in the quest for personal gain, and public spirit, in acquisitiveness.

Thus we Americans are faced with a curious dilemma. We once thought we were going to near the peak of social justice, by giving equality to men through economic liberty. But the very idea itself has intensified the self-interest of the individual to such an extent as to endanger the permanence of the social gains which have been made. Walter Lippmann says:

> We do not have the wisdom and disinterestedness to manage with any assurance the volume of credit which determines the rhythm of the economic enterprise. We do not have the wisdom and disinterestedness to make the world secure against war. We do not have the wisdom and disinterestedness to plan and arrange the growth of our cities or the future of agriculture or the balance between agriculture and industry.

The next plan for the achievement of social justice must solve the problems arising from the absence of wisdom and disinterestedness in our people today.

It is only natural, then, that our political leaders should first think of employing the time-honored method of dealing with acquisitiveness and selfishness, namely, to restrict the liberty of the individual so that he cannot act as he desires. This is what has been done in Russia, in Italy and in Germany. A dictator or an oligarchy take over the government. They prepare their plan for five, ten or more years. By right of military or police power, they limit production, order occupational distribution, and determine hours of labor, wages, and prices. This is the ideal of New America. This is the ideal of the Techno-

LAISSEZ-FAIRE AND EDUCATION 129

crats. The dictator is to be philosopher and king, or to modernize Plato, economist, engineer and king. Such an autocratic check on selfishness may be successful for a time, as long as the genius, if he be a good man, is in power; but experience shows that dictatorships always degenerate into tyranny, and the future holds the certainty that in time conditions will be far worse than before.

The other method of dealing with ignorance and selfishness is to work from within by means of education; to secure wisdom and disinterestedness through the molding of the minds of the young. Wisdom is the goal of all education. It is the delight of scholars. The man who is truly wise thinks little of self; and his taste for the good and his choices of the worth-while guide him steadily. Too much borrowing, too much gambling, too much manufacturing, too much search for gain caused the depression; but there can be no oversupply of philosophy or art, of poetry or drama; nor can there be overproduction of knowledge or of good works.

The trouble with wisdom is that it is so difficult to achieve that only a very few persons in any one generation may be said to acquire it. It is fortunate, therefore, that while disinterestedness flows from wisdom, it is possible to achieve the former without the latter. It was not wisdom alone that built the cathedral at Chartres; it was not wisdom alone that carried Livingstone into darkest Africa; it was not wisdom alone that enabled Washington and his handful of troops to stand off the enemy for eight long years. Whether based in part upon wisdom or not, the moving force was a tremendous interest in something beyond self; and interest of this sort, unlike wisdom, has time and again pervaded whole populations.

The supreme problem for American education is to discover the constituents of this kind of interest, to learn how to adapt it to modern conditions, and to discover the educational milieu most favorable for its inspiration in an entire people. May it not be possible for a modern society to turn all its agencies for research and learning to this task? There is the opportunity to learn what makes men work and do and dare; to explain the enthusiasms of the victorious army, the miracle of Chartres, or Bourges, or Rheims; the personal sacrifice of the missionaries; the spirit of Booker T. Washington or Armstrong or Frissell or Wallace Buttrick, or of thousands of public servants who loved their fellow men and by their love inspired them. Some will say that we need a return to the old religion; others, a revival of the patriotism of our fathers; others, a development of the idea of public responsibility; and still others, a growth of the spirit of service.

So the seekers for social justice find themselves

LAISSEZ-FAIRE AND EDUCATION

at the start of another journey. They have toiled along the road toward democracy. They have climbed the heights of plenty. They are arriving at the destination of laissez-faire. The motives that brought them along this journey, based on self-interest and self-seeking, set free in this new world are about to destroy all the gains that have been made. The forked roads lie ahead. Down one branch lies the planned civilization autocratically arranged to curb the self-interest of ignorant men. Down the other lies democracy, hoping to achieve the same results by education. Which road will America take?

Let us hope that we choose the democratic road; that we have the faith that the motives of men can be remade, that some of our people may gain wisdom, and that we may discover the educational means whereby the enthusiasms of our people may be so aroused and their interests so stimulated that competing and getting and winning and defeating will seem small indeed. Then we shall have the wisdom to plan our future. Then we shall have the disinterestedness to avoid war. It will not be the dictator from without who will compel us, but rather interest and wisdom from within which will lead us. Let us maintain a measure of equality by using the methods of liberty rather than tyranny to control the evils of spirit which liberty and equality themselves have engendered and developed.

VII

IDLENESS—A PROBLEM AND AN OPPORTUNITY

VII

IDLENESS—A PROBLEM AND AN OPPORTUNITY

During the last year of the War I was crossing the Pacific. The old *Empress of Japan,* a very small steamer by current standards, was crowded with returning residents of the Far East,—missionaries, business men, teachers,—who had been held on the coast by the diversion of shipping to carry troops, munitions, and food across the North Atlantic. To this already overloaded vessel had been added a small party of newspaper men, motion picture operators, and publicity agents, who, as representatives of the Committee on Public Information, were voyaging to sell America to the world. The Captain, in search of entertainment and talent for the inevitable ship's concert for the benefit of the widows and orphans of those who sailed the seas, failing to find vaudeville actresses or opera stars, hit upon the motion picture operators, and learned from them that they would gladly assemble a projector and give a show,—provided that the materials could be brought forth from the hold and the films taken from the fireproof vault. To this proposal there was joyous agreement, and the Captain ordered one of the forward holds to be opened and the boxes hoisted out. It was fortunate that the sea was calm, the weather fair and the glass high, for all day long from early morning until sunset, all through the night, and all the next day, some score of men toiled in the hold shifting boxes, barrels, bales, bundles, and crates; all day long and all night engineers rattled the donkey engines, hoisting freight. The forward deck was piled high. Everything was turned over and examined, until away down deep, almost upon the keel, was discovered the boxed cinematograph, triumphantly to be brought to the regions above. It must have been loaded with the first freight. Because of these long hours of toil and struggle, the first class passengers were regaled with "Brown of Harvard," "Scenes in Central Park," and views of "Our Feathered Friends,"—so much labor for so little result. I asked the Captain if he thought the game worth the candle. He replied that it did not make any difference. One of his chief jobs was to keep the crew busy. For emergency purposes, he said, a full crew was needed; that there was little to do in good weather at sea; and that they might as well shift cargo as to paint, scrape and clean. He said that the danger at sea was as great from an idle crew as from fog or storm, and that every ship's captain in the interest of order was compelled to keep

A PROBLEM AND AN OPPORTUNITY 137

every man at work all of his waking time. Without this there would be disorder and discontent.

It seems to me that society in ages past has followed the idea of the Captain of the ship. A few people have been on the top of the pile. The great mass has had only to honor and to obey. By crude processes of manufacture and by ancient and simple modes of agriculture, man has been able to maintain himself by the sweat of his brow; and if by this procedure he has provided his family with food, clothing and shelter, he has generally been content. He may labor from dawn until dark, day after day, year after year. The yield may be sparse; the rewards slight. But he is at work, his wife is at work, the children are at work. There is no mutiny in such a crew. There is no mischief done by idle hands. The society that is at work is secure.

Sometimes the ship comes to port and the men receive shore leave. Here they blow off their steam, but not on board. So in most societies there have been periodic cessations from toil. There is the seventh day of Jews and Christians, the Market Day in the East, Saturnalia, May Day, Christmas, New Year's Day, Easter, the Emperor's Birthday. The farmer leaves his plough, the woodsman abandons his axe, the artisan drops his tools. All change their normal activities. There is a religious rite to attend, a patriotic act to perform, a traditional ceremony in which to participate, an old-time game to play, an ancient tale to hear. Then the ear gives no heed to discontent, no attention is paid to conspiracy. In a secure society people do not idle. They are busy, busy at work, busy at play, busy at initiation ceremonies, busy at war. Idleness they abhor. Lethargy they abominate.

Occasionally as we look into the past, we find illustrations of groups of people who for one reason or another had nothing to do. Take the case of the victorious army one week after its return in triumph from a successfully terminated campaign. The parade is over. The captives have been exhibited; the booty displayed. The enemy's standards are in the museum. What are the soldiers to do? Years on the field of war displace a man from his normal walk of life. He has lived. He has seen. He has marched with Alexander. He has crossed the Rubicon. He has seen the sun at Austerlitz. He has suffered at Valley Forge. He is the idol of youth, the pride of the locality; and he likes to tell about it. How can he settle down to the placid, humdrum work that he used to do? It is so much more pleasant to sit around the stove at the store, tell of the Wheat Field at Gettysburg and meet all the trains. Caesar rewarded his soldiers by grants of land. So did Napoleon. Washington was solicitous that the heroes of the Revolution, away from home for eight long years, should be properly rewarded

A PROBLEM AND AN OPPORTUNITY

with grants of land in the Ohio Valley. It is at least worthy of note that these soldiers' grants were far away,—weeks removed in travel time from the centers of government.

Transportation is not the only method employed by societies troubled by the idle. The unemployed mobs that surged in the streets of Rome were a menace to the security of the State. They had to be fed; and they were fed. They also had to be occupied; and this is the explanation of the coliseums and stadiums in which were held the contests, the races, the massacres, there to divert the idle and unoccupied and hold them in line. I have no doubt, looking at the problem from this point of view, that a part of the toleration of opium and narcotics, widespread drunkenness and gambling, horse races, sweepstakes, and lotteries is due to the fact that these are all diversions for the idle. They may be bad, but they are better than revolution.

Now, in our analysis of the problems of the Power Age we have pointed out that we are likely to face the conditions, dreaded not only by the ship's Captain, but by all societies in the past. It seems almost certain many people will be idle. The youth will not be employed; the middle aged may be retired at forty-five. Men and women during their best years will indulge in brief periods of furious activity to be followed each day by hours of relaxation and two or three days of rest each week. What shall we do? We cannot deport the unemployed. The frontier is gone and the free land taken. We will not tolerate opium. We have neither a body of ancient customs nor a common organized set of religious observances. Most of the usual social medicines devised to control idle crowds are denied to us in the United States. Our one hope is education.

This means, in the first place, that in the Power Age we will have to find something for idle people to do. Making a living will not require much time. More will be given to other pursuits. People will have a chance for fun. Of course, there is pleasure in motion pictures, in the radio or speeding in an automobile; but they are expensive and the appetite becomes jaded. We must direct our education to providing our children with a taste for the real pleasures of life. We should take them far enough along the road, so that of themselves they will continue into the realms of music and art, literature and drama, plays and games, supplementary hobbies and avocations; and even now and then convince a few that a thorough command of some one branch of human knowledge is the greatest pleasure in the world. We adults were prepared to live in a society far different from that in which we are likely to find ourselves tomorrow. We must be re-educated to occupy our leisure time. We must

A PROBLEM AND AN OPPORTUNITY

lock the barn door before all the horses are stolen.

Not only is education the hope which our society has for the proper use of its periods of leisure; but in addition, it is through education that we may be able to soften the blow of the occupational maldistribution and technological unemployment that the future portends.

The government will have to do something about unemployment. It has tried the C.W.A. and the C.C.C. It has embarked upon a vast program of public works. It is projecting a tremendous scheme of unemployment insurance. It is possible that we may use our idle time for an education which will supplement this form of insurance, just as education has served to reduce insurance risks in so many other fields. What is the relation between insurance companies and education? Insurance from that aspect divides itself into two classes. In one class we find insurance such as lightning insurance, tornado insurance, plate-glass insurance, insurance against rain; and in another class life insurance, fire insurance, accident insurance and health insurance. Companies writing policies of the latter type are active educationally. There is fire-prevention propaganda, in which all our people are reminded of the dangers of fire hazards. Accident insurance companies sponsor campaigns for safety and stimulate the teaching of the exercise of caution and care. Most of the life insurance companies have alert educational departments working through the schools, the press, and the radio to teach the public, and incidentally their policy holders, how to guard against disease and how to improve their health. We are all familiar with Good Health Week, Fire Prevention Week, and the Safety Education Association. The insurance companies all play a part in these activities, if they have not actually inspired them; but we never hear of Lightning Week, Tornado Week, nor the Society for the Protection of Plate Glass. You cannot educate against an Act of God.

If then, we of the United States, are to become an insurance company to issue policies against unemployment, we should take a leaf from the book of the insurance companies and if the causes of the insured condition are susceptible of improvement by education, then it would be only good business to carry through a corresponding educational program.

Now the causes of unemployment are diverse. A new machine is invented, and many former operators are thrown out of work. A hundred scattered factories are absorbed in a merger, and concentration of manufacturing closes half of them, or varies the period of operation. High speed machines tend to put emphasis on the younger worker, and help to create the idleness beyond forty-five.

One factor tending to intensify the unemploy-

A PROBLEM AND AN OPPORTUNITY 143

ment problem is frequently noted; namely, the closed frontier. There have always been periods of depression and times when jobs were hard to get. When there was still good land vacant to the west, it was possible for a worker who was no longer regularly employed to take the covered wagon, the axe, the gun and the salt and fare forth. There were difficulties to be met, there were rivers to cross, perils to encounter, and hardships to suffer and obstacles to overcome. It was a step into the unknown, but it gave a chance for a new start in life and reopened the door of hope for fame and fortune. It appealed to all ages. It offered a career despite previous failure, and asked neither special scholastic preparation nor practical experience. It ironed men out. Class lines were left behind. It beckoned men to enter a new race which was to be run from an even start with a free field.

The open frontier with good land free or at low cost was the safety valve of the days that are gone never to return. Can we supply our present deficiency by education? What are the specifications? A new job—a new start in life—a different task—a step into the unknown—rivers to cross—perils to encounter—hardships to suffer—obstacles to overcome—a reopened door of hope for fame and fortune—a career in prospect despite previous failure, lack of scholastic preparation or inexperience—banishment of class lines—

an equal opportunity. Is there anything that corresponds with this prescription? It seems to me that it is a good definition of American education itself, and particularly of formal adult education.

There is a frontier without and a frontier within. Now that the external frontier is closed and its good lands occupied, we can turn to the frontier within, which never can be closed. In occupying this new frontier, we should be mindful of the allures of the old West; the different job and the new start, the obstacles to be overcome, the equality of opportunity, and the reopened door of hope for fame and fortune. These should be the standards for adult reëducation.

Somewhere in the total educational program these specifications should be met. They involve an effort to bring up young men and women to be versatile. They include a possibility of emphasizing the second string to the bow. Perhaps every American citizen should have an alternative vocation which at first might serve as a recreation, such as gardening, cabinet-making, fishing, trapping, or skill at some of the remaining processes of manufacture that are carried on in the home, which might serve as a refuge at a time of illness or mental distress and in time of unemployment become a foundation for a new start.

The proper occupation of the frontier within involves also a thoroughly worked out plan of

A PROBLEM AND AN OPPORTUNITY 145

vocational repreparation or retraining. Just as in frontier days when anyone could go, so now anyone able to walk mentally should be allowed to fare forth; and we should be very careful to see to it that the doors are open equally to all. There are difficulties today,—costs of education, expenses for care of family and temporary meager standards of living;—but these obstacles, like the Indians, the tornadoes and the blizzards, can be overcome if only there is hope for the future. We could have state and national financial assistance. We now have a farm loan board that helps the farmer to get a start. We might have a vocational education loan fund to help workers to get another start. If we are likely to have unemployment insurance payments for an indefinite time in the future, it might be good business for the American people to discount these by advanced grants in aid of reëducation.

The drift of the argument by now is clear and needs no further elaboration. Extended unemployment is supposed to be a characteristic of the age into which we are entering. Governmental unemployment insurance seems likely to be adopted by all of the states. Possibly the cost of this remedy may be largely decreased, if like other insurance companies, we resort to education, partially to diminish the causes which make it necessary.

We have shown how the approach of the

Power Age has vastly complicated the problem of liberty and equality; how tremendous economic inequalities have forced the government toward dictatorship; how self-interest and intense competition are forcing an abandonment of laissez-faire. It was suggested in each case that there was a possibility of compromise between the extreme positions by a new education; an education as yet undeveloped, but certainly tremendously difficult. This new education will be a task of great magnitude. It will be impossible to accomplish in the few hours a day, the few weeks a year and the few years of the ordinary school. It will mean education extended into adult life. It will mean education for all the people, no matter where they live. Education cannot be advanced at one place and backward at another. Ignorance at any point, however remote, will be a source of danger. It is fortunate therefore, that the Power Age which has caused all these difficulties, has brought with it the possibility of their solution, in extended leisure or in general unemployment. It will be our great opportunity.

Education may have a further function. The social forces now at work may be driving society in a direction which may prove to be intolerable. Because new processes are devised and new inventions made, because a whole new life develops on earth, it does not follow that mankind should

A PROBLEM AND AN OPPORTUNITY

forever accept the kind of society which he happens to find. We have in our educational system an instrument which man, if he so minds, may use to direct his own destiny, a force by means of which society may reshape itself. Slaves to the machine we need not be. So in every consideration of the implications for education of the Power Age, we have the right, even the duty, to consider not only the problem of how to train man so that he may live in this new society, but also how to inspire him so that he may, if need be, change this new society into one in which it is good to live. This is the more important question, and as such should command our constant attention.

There is one further implication. Bad times should be busy times in education. If the contention of this argument is well founded, education should redouble its strength when economic conditions are bad. The life insurance company during an influenza epidemic does not cut down its educational department, or effect economies by combining jobs or restricting material supplies. When automobile accidents increase, the casualty companies do not on that account cease their propaganda for safety in driving and teaching the rules of the road; but when people are out of work and incomes are cut, the tendency is all in the direction of decreasing expenditures for education. This is poor business and it will prove to be a false economy in the long run. When seas roll high and tempests blow we need new sails and strong rigging. This is the time when the educator is needed; and if we would avoid the day of communism as one possibility, or fascism as another, or the apple seller and the beggar as a third, we must turn to education as a social vaccination against industrial ills. If we are competent and know what we are doing, if we can plan wisely and judge what is to come, if we are able to put into practice what we know to be right, then in good conscience can we bend our best efforts to extend education to every child, youth and adult, secure in the knowledge that we are advocating increased support of an activity that is neither luxurious, minor, nor peripheral, but is rather the prime and central concern of a bewildered society striving to adjust itself to the complexities of the Power Age.

VIII

LIBERTY, EQUALITY, AND NATIONAL EDUCATION

VIII

LIBERTY, EQUALITY, AND NATIONAL EDUCATION

If it is true that education should be the prime concern of a bewildered society trying to adjust itself to the complexities of the Power Age; if it is true that liberty and equality, sought for since the founding of the republic, will perish from the earth, unless we effect the proper compromises through education; then it is high time, that we the people, begin to look upon our public schools and universities as a national concern; and work out some plan whereby their financing at least will not be left to the unequal resources of localities and states, and their general ideals to the whims and vagaries of isolated communities.

We have known for many years past; indeed, it has now become generally accepted that we cannot trust the education of American children to the sum of money available from the resources of a small taxing district, nor to the social ideals of a backward, illiterate community. I remember once being conducted on a tour of inspection of the rural schools in Shelby County, Tennessee;

traveling over smooth roads, past prosperous farms, to beautiful consolidated schools, each with ample grounds, assembly halls, laboratories for home economics and agriculture, attended by well-dressed children, presided over by trained, experienced and well-paid teachers. At one point we crossed the county line; the paving stopped; down a rutted dirt road we came to a small stream, with no bridge, and hub deep in water, spraying on all sides, we crossed to the other bank, slid through the mud, and drove up beside a rickety school, unpainted, with cracks, knotholes, dirty windowpanes surrounding the gaps left by those long since vanished. No sanitary arrangements, meager equipment, bare feet and overalls.

Experiences of this kind are convincing. Those who cannot make many trips like this may travel vicariously; and those who cannot gather the proper perspective from many visits may have the facts assembled and presented to them. Survey, tables and statistics are the methods we in education use to give travelogues to the many. By averages we paint the picture, by standard deviations we tell the story; and in many a report or study, or in the dry dust of financial surveys, my experience near Memphis has been repeated. We note riches in one district, destitution in another; many children in one, few in another; great wealth and few children in one; poverty

LIBERTY, EQUALITY AND EDUCATION

and many children in another. A melting glacier ages ago leaves a moraine, an ancient lake dammed by the ice deposits fertile soil on its bed, a torrent surging erodes a wide area; Mother Nature deposits oil at one place and iron ore at another; a legislature allocates railroad taxes according to main line track mileage; and American children in 1936, on those accounts, are provided with or deprived of opportunities for education. With a given effort in proportion to real wealth, one community furnishes a hovel for a school building, a short school term, a poorly trained teacher and ancient textbooks. In another, there is a modern fire-proof school, a long term, a trained teacher, adequate laboratories, splendid equipment, motion pictures, and radios, and the school board could easily give each graduate a trip to Washington and a gold watch. It was this problem that Cubberley, Elliott, Strayer and Updegraff attacked a generation ago. It was this problem that awaited Mort's researches for a plan of action. It is this problem that Maryland and Delaware, New York and Ohio, North Carolina and New Jersey, Pennsylvania and many other states are in process of solving. It is to be hoped that in the not far distant future, the welfare of any child within the boundaries of any one state will no longer depend upon happenings in geological history, upon accidents of legislative injustice, upon the chances of racial origin, upon the operations of local prejudice, upon the prevalence of hookworm or trachoma. The struggle for state equalization of educational opportunity is on the way to victory. Sometime in the not too far distant future every one of the forty-eight states will have adopted a plan for equalization of educational opportunity and the state financing of a recognized minimum program.

But even then the battle will not be won. Just as mere inspection and scientific investigation reveal inequalities within the states, so there is variation of educational opportunity among the states themselves. We are all familiar with the data presented by Leonard P. Ayres, with the reports presented by the Bureau of Education, with the facts gathered by the National Education Association, with the interpretations made by Norton and Mort. Norton shows that the twelve richest states are more than three times as able to meet their educational obligations as the twelve poorest, and that California is probably six times as well off as Mississippi. I do not need to dwell upon the wealth of evidence tending to reveal the disparities among the states. Sometime when a proper national study of school finance is carried to completion, the full facts will be known. It is obvious that great educational injustices will be revealed, inequalities in ability to pay, and that these difficulties will be remedied only when a far larger proportion of

LIBERTY, EQUALITY AND EDUCATION

school revenue comes from the nation as a whole. We cannot reënact an Act of God, but we can adjust ourselves to the inequalities of Nature.

There has been inequality amongst the states from the start. We should have had national financial aid to the schools from the beginning. But the need has increased rather than decreased with each succeeding year. When the bulk of the wealth was in real property, there was a rough and relatively steady relation between the location of taxable wealth and the location of educational expenditures. A factory brought wealth to a town. It also brought many children. Wealth was scattered on the farms. So were the prospective pupils. Inadequate as the general property tax may have been in an agrarian civilization, it has become definitely worse as we live in the Machine Age and approach the Power Age. No longer are our wants supplied locally. We buy our automobiles from Detroit, our tires from Ohio, our iron from Pennsylvania and Indiana. Chain stores cover the nation. Capital has become concentrated in New York, in Chicago, in Boston; and wealth which should help support schools in Arkansas and Mississippi goes to Brookline, Bronxville and Evanston. I shall make no categorical statement. I know that economists disagree upon this point. I assert without proof at this moment that the concentration of capital in the Machine and Power economies has increased the disparities in the abilities of the states to support education by means of the taxing systems now commonly in use. Only in the nation as a whole does the power rest. Nor need I mention the inequality caused by the haphazard manner in which coal, iron, silver, oil and other mineral resources were long ago deposited in our soil. Minnesota children have no more right to profit from the Mesabi Range, or Texas children from the oil fields, than New York children have to profit from the Erie Canal, the great harbor and the concentration of railroads and shipping. National aid must come.

Federal aid to the schools is no new policy. The Confederation, legislating for the National Domain in 1785, set aside land for schools, and in 1787 evinced a national concern for education. Beginning with the acts of 1802 and 1803 and continuing in greater detail just prior to the admission of each succeeding state, the Congress of the United States has granted aid to education in general and also to particular institutions. With the first Morrill Act of 1862 federal aid was given to special institutions, the land-grant colleges; and the Hatch Act in 1887, supporting the experiment stations, put the government directly at work in state institutions. The Adams Act of 1906 and the Purnell Act of 1925 gave additional appropriations to and placed new restrictions upon these experiment stations. The

LIBERTY, EQUALITY AND EDUCATION

second Morrill Act of 1890 and the Nelson Amendment of 1907 gave more land to the land-grant colleges, gave them in addition annual subsidies in cash, and placed more power in government hands by enabling the government to withhold funds. The first grant for special education, together with the first appearance of the idea of requiring the state to match federal funds came with the Marine School Act of 1911. Federal aid to stimulate special subjects in the common schools (in this case agriculture and home economics) came with the Smith-Lever Act of 1914 and the Smith-Hughes Act of 1917, the Civilian Vocational Rehabilitation Acts of 1920, 1924 and 1930; and the George-Reed Act of 1929 gave direct federal subsidy to vocational education, with much governmental direction and considerable control. In 1930 the Federal government paid to the states more than $20,000,000 in support of these projects.

The Federal government has also coöperated with the states in many other matters. It has made payments to the states from its national forest funds, in its coöperative fire prevention service, in forest planting, in the construction of rural post roads, in the promotion of welfare and hygiene of maternity, in supplying printed materials for the blind, in providing homes for disabled soldiers and sailors, and in subsidizing the National Guard. In 1930 the sum total for these agencies totalled nearly six times the subsidies for education.

The need for national aid to the states, apparent from the start and increased by commercial developments of the Power Age, became critical during the depression. Inequalities once bearable became intolerable in many communities. In one locality, dependence is upon a single crop, wheat or tobacco, corn or cotton. The market drops out of sight. So do the schools. In another locality, we find that a notoriously bad system of banking law and practice causes financial chaos; and the schools collapse. Here there is a struggle between a city, a county and a state legislature which causes taxes to go unpaid for one—two—three years; and a Century of Progress culminates in a broken-down school system, a demoralized student body and a teaching force ready for any mischief.

It is not the schools alone that are affected by a depression. All the ordinary agencies of agriculture, commerce and industry are seriously hurt, and into the breach has stepped the Federal government. With the legislation of the last years of the Hoover Administration, and in the first one hundred days of "The New Deal," we find a new national policy. The Reconstruction Finance Corporation, a private corporation backed by the government, has loaned huge sums to banks, to railroads, to private enterprises of

LIBERTY, EQUALITY AND EDUCATION 159

all sorts. Under the Roosevelt Administration we see not only a large national undertaking in the development of the Tennessee Valley, but we are promised huge "public works," furnishing employment for hundreds of thousands. These projects include ships for the navy, buildings for the government, waterworks, roads, sewerage systems, dams, bridges and the like. Why then has the Federal government failed to act in aid of Education? Largely, I think because of the continuance of an old tradition. For the school system has always been "dear to the hearts of the American people" and closely responsive to their ideals.

Those who believed in *liberty* have always wanted to determine the education of their own children and they have ever been reluctant to delegate the power to anyone else. They retained the church school; they supported private schools; and despite the growing tendency to depend upon the state and federal governments they have, in the main, kept the control and support of education in the localities. Such state control as does exist developed not so much from direct delegation by the people as from the acceptance of grants the strings to which were not too apparent at the start. For the most part the people in a locality in the United States still pick the teacher they want, pay him what they please, tell him what to teach and what books he shall use, place him in the kind of school building they choose, and discharge him when they get ready. They assert their right to do this as a part of the liberty in which our country believes and they desire no important encroachment upon their prerogative to determine what their children shall be like when they grow up. This is a definite purpose of American society and our school system has tried to adjust itself to it.

Those who believed in *equality,* however, even in the early days, soon saw that equality of opportunity could not be provided if children were to have the kind of education that a particular community could financially afford to provide. They saw rich districts and poor districts, wealthy counties and impoverished counties, side by side. They urged an increase in the size of the taxing unit, reform and often complete change in the system of state distribution of school funds, and the entrance of the Federal government as a source of support for schools. The American people have not been content to allow the citizens of ill-favored communities to stagger under a tax burden which at best will provide only a short term under a poorly paid teacher in a squalid building, while others in wealthy areas are able to provide splendid opportunities with little effort. Increased participation of larger governmental units in the financing of local educational pro-

LIBERTY, EQUALITY AND EDUCATION

grams is apparently a settled policy of American government. The purpose is to foster equality.

Nor have the American people been content to allow their children to be at the mercy of the particular educational ambitions of the locality. Larger governmental units have interfered to say that a school must be provided whether the home folks want it or not; that it must be open for so many days; that the teacher must have at least certain qualifications and be paid not less than so much and that the building must be safe and warm. Sometimes there have been direct orders. More often the state government or the federal government has offered monetary prizes if a particular condition is met. Here, also, the purpose is to secure equality.

We see in these developments a curious conflict in American educational practices; yet there is nothing mysterious about it. It comes from the effort to adapt American education to the two different ideals, the ideal of liberty and the ideal of equality. For many years this growing conflict was not apparent, the changes took place so slowly; but in the last decade it has become perfectly evident. Measures, which have been introduced into Congress to create a government department dealing with education, to be presided over by an officer who would be a member of the President's cabinet, have divided the country into two camps.

The advocates of these measures are the men and women who believe primarily in *equality*. They have seen the failure of the small locality. They know that equal school terms, reasonably adequate physical facilities, proper teachers, and adequate equipment are impossible without assistance from larger governmental units and they know that children in many places need protection against the prejudices, social peculiarities, and dulled ambitions that seem to center about infertile land, rocky hills, and remote regions. If it is logical for the state to protect the child from the locality and to equalize the wealth, it is just as logical that upon occasions the nation must protect the child from the state.

The opponents of these measures are the adherents of *liberty*. They want equality, but not at the expense of liberty. They desire no encroachment by the Federal government, no weakening of local authority. They assert that it is proper for the state to assume more power; but not for the nation. They fear centralization of the kind found in Australia or France and they want to be sure that the minds of the children of America will never be in the power of the political group that happens, at any time, to be in control at Washington. Their arguments are strengthened by recent events in Germany, Russia, and Italy; and the public resentment at the efforts of certain public utility corporations to

LIBERTY, EQUALITY AND EDUCATION 163

influence the schools gives a clue to the attitude of the people. In short, when we consider equality, participation by the federal government in education seems desirable; when we take liberty into account, there seems to be danger.

There is a way out of this dilemma. The trouble lies not in the inevitable opposition of the ideals, but in the unwarranted assumption that education, school administration, educational control are all of one piece, solid, and incapable of division. This is not true.

In Europe there is a division of school administration that is universally understood and so generally accepted that one fails to find a definition or explanation. It is accepted as though no other attitude were ever considered. In the law, in official handbooks, in textbooks we find reference to the "interna" and the "externa"; internal and external administration of schools. Internal has to do with what is taught, how it is taught, how the teacher is trained, and the life and spirit of the school. External deals with seeing that the pupils attend, providing suitable places for instruction, keeping the school building clean and habitable, the pupils well, the teachers paid, the equipment provided. The chalk that the teacher uses is external; what he writes with the chalk, internal. His salary is external; what he teaches and the way he does it, internal. That the pupil shall be given glasses so that he may read is external; what he reads is internal. The pupils march out of the building to study plants in the garden; this is internal. The janitor walks into the building to fire the stove; this is external. The material side of education is external; the spiritual and mental side is internal. So commonly is this concept accepted in Europe that different school officials are assigned to each; and in general the external is controlled and supported by government units different from those controlling and supporting the internal.

France and England present an interesting illustration of this. In France the "interna" are completely controlled by Paris and the "externa" on the other hand by the locality, although this latter control grows less year by year. The Minister of Education controls the textbooks and the course of study. Orders go forth from his office with the force of law. He trains, appoints, and promotes all school teachers and officials. Even disciplinary and social problems are settled under his direction. The departments and the communes, however, have the power to erect school buildings, to provide janitor service, to see to it that the children attend, to select a school doctor, to provide living quarters for the teacher, to beautify school grounds, and the like. The locality can in no way determine what shall be taught; but it may see to it that the child is ready to be taught. This is generally termed a

LIBERTY, EQUALITY AND EDUCATION

highly centralized system; but it is plain to be seen that it is centralized in part and decentralized in part.

In England, on the other hand, we see almost precisely the reverse. The borough, the urban district, or the county through the education committee of its council has complete control of the internal administration of the schools. No person in London orders what shall be taught, how it shall be taught, or who shall teach it. This is in the power of the local unit, and often it is delegated to the small community and sometimes to the school itself. The Englishman believes in liberty. Nevertheless the President of the Board of Education, usually termed the Minister of Education outside of England, is a member of the government. Parliament, from the national treasury, pays more than half the cost of education. The Board has a good deal to say about length of the school term, attendance of pupils, buildings, salaries, pensions, and physical education. As to the internal phases it can do no more than suggest; but since the suggestions are the result of careful research and world-wide investigation, they receive thoughtful attention. This is generally termed a decentralized system; but it is plain to be seen that it is decentralized only in part.

This division of school administration points the way, as I see it, to the solution of the American problem. We need centralization to provide equality; we fear centralization as a menace to our liberty. Very well! Let us agree to centralize the externals, reserving to the localities complete control over the internals. Let us state with such exactness that we shall never be misunderstood that we propose in our state governments, and if necessary in the nation, to centralize the financing of education, the material side of schooling, and the responsibility for investigation and research; reserving to the localities the right to determine in the last analysis what shall be taught and how. Keep teacher training as decentralized as possible. Then we shall see to it that every child is given a chance without the danger of placing the control of the American mind within the reach of a partisan group. We can have equality and liberty both.

It is said that "he who pays the piper calls the tune." There is undoubtedly the danger, as is seen in the development of the Federal Board for Vocational Education, that efforts to provide financial assistance are apt to carry with them dictation on the part of central authorities over internals. This has also been seen in the various states. I think that many measures adopted by state legislatures as they affect the content of the course of study are dangerous to the liberties of the American people. The Tennessee anti-evolution law is only one illustration. We pride ourselves, however, that we have a government of

LIBERTY, EQUALITY AND EDUCATION

laws, not of men; and may we not, as in England, be able definitely to prescribe in law some automatic basis of state and federal participation which will carry no discretionary power with it? England has done it; I see no reason why we cannot.

Our development in the United States to the present time seems to provide equality in the state governments without liberty; and liberty in the federal government without equality. It is to be hoped that by far-sighted legislation we shall be able to take a different step, not by a selection of one to the exclusion of the other, not by a dull and inadequate compromise, but by a centralization in the state and federal government of the externals and a decentralization of the internals. It seems to be easily possible; and I can see no reason why proponents and opponents alike could not join hands in such a program which would look to the realization in the life of tomorrow of the ideals for which our country was founded and for which so much sacrifice has been made. It would sever from the national and state governments powers which threaten the liberties of the people; and it would render unto the state and nation power making for equality of opportunity. It would also give us the financial basis for a system of education which with a firm and steady step could march forward to play its part in saving liberty and equality from the onslaughts of the Power Age.

IX

THE WORLD OF THOUGHT

"In studying the birth of ideas, or at least their metamorphoses; in following them from their feeble beginnings, as they grow and develop, . . . through their progress and successive victories to their final triumph; one comes to the profound conviction that it is intellectual and moral force, not material, that commands and directs life."

HAZARD, *La Crise de la Conscience Européenne.*
I, p. viii.

IX

THE WORLD OF THOUGHT

We now come to the close of this consideration of liberty and equality. We started by showing the government of the United States in 1935, standing between two sets of critics, those who wanted liberty more than equality and those who wanted equality more than liberty. We discussed the conflict between the two ideals. In sketchy fashion we traced their development through history, and showed how eagerly they were desired, and how long their achievement on earth had been delayed. It is our fortune that the Fathers of America made the effort to achieve liberty and equality in real life; and we followed their efforts to bring them into being, now emphasizing the one, now the other. We saw how the Industrial Revolution, 1800–1830, intensified the conflict between the liberals and the equalitarians; how education made the compromise; and we have seen the conflict reappear, this time in very serious form, as a result of our second and more drastic social change, the coming of the Power Age. Liberty appears about to vanish before dictatorship and oligarchy, and laissez-faire before a planned economy. We have discussed the possible function of further compromise through education. Fortunately the Power Age is bringing the possibility of solution along with its problems, for extended leisure or idleness will give the possibility of extended education to all. We can provide this education only if we have a system of schools and colleges, and agencies of adult education, good from north to south and from east to west, and this can come only with national support. We have shown how this goal, long advocated by the equalitarians, long blocked by the liberals, can be achieved in harmony with both of the ideals.

It may be that the compromises I have suggested are too visionary. It may be that the progress toward dictatorship and government control of economic life has gone so far, that it is too late to modify or turn back. Equality may drive liberty from the scene, and we may have a state approaching communism. Or liberty may triumph over equality, and we may return to the old days, with even greater disparities of wealth and influence. Or liberty and equality may both die, and we may grow more like the Empire in the Orient.

If these times come, and education fails to correct the conditions of the material world there is still some hope. For there will still be a world where all men are equal and a world where all

THE WORLD OF THOUGHT

men are free, the world of art and music, of literature and philosophy, the world of science. Spinoza ground lenses all day. Turgot made his most famous contribution by working at night in village inns between trips of inspection. In the Power Age, we may be forced to turn a crank all morning, or tend a machine, or take orders from some functionary at Washington; but that does not mean that we may not be free and equal in the world of the intellect. The passport to this happy land is a liberal education; and with the wealth and leisure of the Power Age, this can be the privilege of all.

What we shall become in the future, depends in the last analysis on what we want. If we want something fiercely enough, we shall get it. Our fathers wanted both liberty and equality. What do we want?

"I am convinced," said Gladstone, "that the welfare of mankind does not now depend upon the state or the world of politics; the real battle is being fought in the world of thought."